"Rowland helps to remind us that mission is not simply one activity of the church, alongside several other equally important activities. But instead, God's mission is the organizing principle of everything we do as followers of Jesus. If you want to better understand what it looks like to engage God's redemptive mission in the places you live, work, and play, then read this book."
—**Brad Brisco,** author of *ReThink: 9 Paradigm Shifts for Activating the Church,* and co-author of *Next Door as It Is in Heaven* and *Missional Essentials*

"Embracing a life of simple mission is both profound and beautiful. In *Life Out Loud,* Rowland plots a course into that life, entreating us to stop being afraid and to do what we know we can do, and be who we know we were meant to be. It is a kind of invitation that reminded me, on every page, of Jesus."
—**Brian Sanders,** executive director, Tampa Underground Network

"Rowland has gifted his readers with a biographical journey into what faith beyond the Sunday experience can look like. This book is full of practical wisdom and missional insights gained through daring to follow Jesus into the spaces and places where God calls us. In the process Rowland provides us with a wonderful example of what it means to be a vulnerable, winsome, honest and loving leader."
—**Alan and Debra Hirsch**, missional leaders; authors and speakers

"This book is both inspiring and convicting: I loved it and it wrecked me at the same time! Rowland has chosen to stay engaged with the church and to shape the missional imagination and practices of many around him. This is going to shape hearts, minds, and paradigms. I dare you to read this!"

—**Alan Briggs,** leadership coach; pastor; author of *Everyone's a Genius* and *Staying Is the New Going*

"For those wanting to live as viral kingdom agents, Rowland has given us a very usable practitioner's guide. *Life Out Loud* both touches and strums our heartstrings: it not only taps into our aspiration to live a life that matters, it gives us some clear ways to do it!"

—**Reggie McNeal**, author of *Kingdom Come* and *Kingdom Collaborators*

"Early on in my journey of following Jesus I often wondered if 'life and life to the full' was in fact a real possibility. In the last several years of my life I have come to realize that not only is it possible, but it is found and experienced when I participate in the exciting and everyday work of God. What Rowland writes is a compelling invitation to experience this full life. *Life Out Loud* is filled with practical ways to join God in his work as well as beautiful stories that inspire us into action. Are you bored, stuck, or stalled in your faith? Do yourself a favor and pick this book up. You will be captivated and caught up into living a louder life."

—**Ryan Hairston**, national director, Forge America

"*Life Out Loud* is a breath of fresh air for those who intuitively know that there is more to the Christian life than simply 'going to church.' Rowland skillfully weaves together profound truths about Christian identity and purpose with real-life stories in ways that engage both the intellect and, perhaps more importantly, the heart. His intent is to inspire you to ask loud questions, take some risks, and live into a more meaningful life as you join Jesus at work in your community."
—**Dr. Mark Hopkins**, director of MA in Global Leadership and the Doctor of Missiology, School of Intercultural Studies, Fuller Theological Seminary

"As a pastor, I wrestle with how I am living and leading others into the call of Christ. I think Rowland is on to a path of life that cuts to the heart of the life Jesus called us to follow. This is a great guidebook for moving from mere motion to true meaning."
—**Thomas Thompson**, senior pastor, Pulpit Rock Church, Colorado Springs, Colorado

"Rowland is pioneering new ways of being the church out and among a culture that is no longer willing to go to church. *Life Out Loud* is a compelling collection of personal stories and practical insights gained on his courageous journey outside the walls of Sunday-centered spirituality. Anyone who has ever sat in a service and wondered 'Is this all there is to the Christian life?' will find new inspiration in these pages!"
—**Jon Ritner**, lead pastor, Ecclesia Hollywood

"In *Life Out Loud*, Rowland gets beyond cliché to clarity by challenging long-held assumptions of what it means to be Christian, human, fashioned in the *imago Dei*. Readers will find this disruptive book soundly framed by practical theology, personal reflection, and experiential knowledge...just the right blend of dirt and divine."

—**Dr. Mark DeYmaz**, founder, Mosaic Church of Central Arkansas; co-founder, Mosaix Global Network; author of *Disruption: Repurposing the Church to Redeem the Community*

"In missional literature there tends to be either theorist or practitioner. Every once in a while you read something with both. Rowland's book is just such a rarity. Read it to learn. Read it to grow. Read it to do."

—**Eric Sandras**, PhD, author of *Buck Naked Faith* and *When the Sky Is Falling*

"One of the great challenges for the church today is to move from a consumer to missional DNA, from attractional services to personal transformation. I'm grateful for Rowland and his call for us to become a relational family who love God and others, always living on mission."

—**Dr. John Sowers**, co-founder and president of The Mentoring Project; author of *The Heroic Path*

"*Life Out Loud* is a refreshing read that lightens the religious load while anchoring you to the weight and depth of gospel living. If the 'church' is truly the people of God, then this book will guide you outside the church...for the sake of the church."
—**Hugh Halter**, author of *Flesh* and co-author of *The Tangible Kingdom*

"In Compassion's work to inspire Christ-followers to live out holistic mission, we regularly sense and see a craving among Christ-followers in North America for a faith that is deeper and wider than simply consuming a once-weekly Sunday service experience. *Life Out Loud* speaks directly to that yearning, boldly inviting Christ-followers to stop 'warming the pews' and instead proclaim and demonstrate the kingdom with our whole life. It is a challenging and important message that I am confident will invigorate and inspire many to a renewed way of living."
—**Allison Alley**, president-elect, Compassion Canada

LIFE
OUT
LOUD

Ann —
Live out loud for
the Kingdom!

Rowland
John 20:21

LIFE
OUT
LOUD

Joining Jesus Outside the Walls of the Church

ROWLAND SMITH

First published in 2019 by 100Movements Publishing
www.100mpublishing.com

ISBN 978-0-9986393-4-5

Edited by Anna Robinson and David Zimmerman
Proofread by Alexa Tewkesbury and Helen Bearn

Cover design by David Provolo

For Kitty, my wife, friend, and partner,
and our children, Carson, Will, Kitty, and Jia

This wild journey following Jesus is not just mine,
but ours as a family
...it will continue.

Acknowledgments

To Kitty—this missional life we now live is as much your birthright as mine. We continue to experience a wild ride following God together, not always easy, but full with stories of God's presence on the dusty road we travel together.

To our children, Carson, and his bride Corrie, Will, Kitty, and Jia—you all inspire me!

To Mike Frost, Alan and Deb Hirsch, and all of the Forge tribe. Over the years, you have been an instrument of God moving me from passivity to actively announcing his kingdom in my own life. I value your friendship and partnership in the kingdom work into which we've all been called. Thank you for inviting me into "The Tribe."

To Alan Briggs and your endless call to lead well, take risks, and pursue kingdom entrepreneurship. You are a wise coach and friend. Thank you for being instrumental in shaping my voice in this book, along with David Zimmerman. You both have pushed me to new frontiers and new ways of thinking.

To Anna Robinson—you are more than an editor. You have been a godsend in helping me shape the thoughts that flow from my heart and my story. My voice as a writer is partly yours, and so you share these pages with me as a storyteller. Thank you!

To the communities of Ecclesia Colorado Springs and Pulpit Rock Church. You know who you are, and are too many to name, but we are chasing God's mission together, and you have been inspirational in your tenacity to see the kingdom expand in Colorado Springs and around the world.

To our Third Space Coffee team past and present—you are so much more than employees or staff! Together we have built a place of community for the city and the neighborhood. Each week hundreds of stories and journeys are intersecting at the café tables and couches in our space. You help curate those spaces well. Thank you for your love of coffee and even larger love of people.

To Cindy Limbrick—words are not enough to express the ironic paths we experience in life together. You're more than a friend: you are a fellow sojourner. I still remember the pivotal night at your kitchen table with our beloved Chuck, as Kitty and I shared with you both the vision God had given us, wading into deep missional waters. Thank you for your friendship, your artistry, your help with designing Third Space, and for speaking life into dreams, including mine.

To the many family and friends I've not named here, not because you are forgotten. The landscape this book covers is whole life, and so everyone I know and love has a part in the shaping of it. I am a blessed person with a host of great people around me. Thank you for walking with me.

Contents

Foreword

We've become used to the term "nones" to describe those who have no religious affiliation or faith, but Josh Packard, the author of a University of Northern Colorado study, recently coined the term "dones" to describe those former churchgoers who nevertheless maintain their faith in God and their Christian identity. And according to his research, this describes an estimated thirty million Americans. Not only that, Packard says there are another seven million "almost dones" coming up behind them.

People are leaving the church in droves, especially so-called millennials. But the picture that seems to be emerging isn't a simple one of wholescale church decline. Part of what is happening is that many committed Christians are continuing to pursue their faith outside institutional church membership. Indeed, Packard's research suggests many of the "dones" felt they needed to leave *in order* to continue to follow Christ. When he asked them why they had left church, he found the top four reasons were:

- they wanted community…and got judgment
- they wanted to affect the life of the church… and got bureaucracy
- they wanted conversation…and got doctrine

● they wanted meaningful engagement with the world…
and got moral prescription.[1]

Clergy who dismiss church leavers as faithless or lazy clearly don't understand the complexities of the situation. There are important lessons for church leaders to learn from the "dones," if only they had the grace to listen.

In this book, Rowland Smith describes his own journey as an "almost done," a gifted worship leader and preacher who had grown bored with the incomplete and unsatisfying rhythm of religion his church experience offered. He wanted to feel like following God was an adventure, but instead he was burdened with the stultifying effects of judgment, bureaucracy, busyness, and doctrinaire morality.

But rather than wandering the religious landscape, forgotten and unaccounted for by the church as many "dones" do, Rowland began a journey to the *center* of the church. He discovered that community, conversation and meaningful engagement were in fact the very stuff of a true church. And along the way he realized that Jesus' plan for his people was for an exciting and momentous adventure, a life lived out loud.

Indeed, Josh Packard's research into the "dones" revealed that the kind of church they desired wasn't that different to Christ's original intention. Packard wrote:

---

1 Josh Packard and Ashleigh Hope, *Church Refugees: Sociologists reveal why people are DONE with church but not their faith* (Group Publishing, 2015), 17.

more than anything what the dechurched want is a home in the truest sense of the word. A place that's safe and supportive and refreshing and challenging. An identifiable place, embedded in a larger community where they both know and are known by those around them and where they feel they can have a meaningful impact on the world. They long for the same kind of church that we all long for. They desire a church that's active and engaged with the world, where people can bring their full and authentic selves and receive love and community in return.[2]

In *Life Out Loud*, Rowland Smith writes not as a researcher, but as a case study. He has walked the same road as the "dones" and "almost dones." But he's found that rather than simply confining the practice of faith to a weekly worship gathering and a midweek meeting, the meaningful life Jesus wants for you is found primarily in the places you live, work, and play. That is, outside the church walls. And you don't need to leave church to find it. You can *be* the church in the world, just as Jesus promised.

I've seen Rowland at work in his coffee shop, Third Space Coffee. I've joined him in his work of linking the church and the city of Colorado Springs in one of the most exciting ecumenical movements of community engagement and Christian service I've seen. I've partnered with him in training others in

---

2 Ibid., 21.

these principles through the Forge Mission Training Network. I've been led in worship by him. I've eaten at his family's dinner table. The guy is the real deal, and this book is a beautiful record of his journey in rediscovering himself as a sent person, and joining Jesus in living a loud life, not quietly sitting in the back pew, but launching forth to alert others to the exciting life Christ offers.

If you're done with church and just want a privatized faith of sorts, a warm sense of God's vague presence deep down in your heart somewhere, this book isn't for you. If part of your frustration with institutional religion involves a nagging feeling that there's got to be more to following Jesus than just attending meetings, then read on. Rowland has been on this loud and meaningful adventure for a while now, and he knows the way out. Turn the next page and start the daring peregrination with him.

Michael Frost,
Morling College, Sydney

Preface

I remember the day Mark told me he was leaving the church.

We'd played and written music together in my early days as a Christian. I was in my late twenties, and our songs were mostly about our faith journey and Jesus. We recorded an album, pitched to record labels, and hoped it might even become a career. We made a good team: his lyrics contained foundational biblical truths from growing up in the church, and my not-raised-in-church phrases and guitar riffs made our music more culturally relevant. We never "made it," but to this day I still enjoy some of the songs we crafted and have fond memories of the journey we shared.

Mark wasn't leaving Jesus. He was just leaving the institution. The business of church had dampened his faith, and he needed to seek a way of practicing that brought life back into his walk with Jesus. His initial plan was to spend Sundays in the mountains of Arkansas, canoeing streams, or camping. He felt that being in creation would reorient himself toward God. For him, God had left the building. And so he needed to find him again. Something was absent from his Sunday morning attendance: it somehow felt incomplete. He was bored, unenthusiastic, running on a hamster wheel of religion.

His experience is not unique. Mark's outlook is becoming

common among many people sitting in the pews of church buildings today, and it's only increasing. Perhaps you're feeling an urge to nod your head in agreement. This disillusionment is not a tsunami wave of discontent; rather the tide is coming in slowly but surely. More and more people are bored with their faith and are left wondering if church attendance is all there is.

There have been numerous studies documenting how many people are leaving the constructs of organized church and institutional religion. For them, the church is irrelevant to discussions about twenty-first-century life, immaterial to their life at all. They see the church as antagonistic to contemporary culture and rarely consider it a valid voice. Sadly, this number is on the rise. These are the "nones" Mike referred to in the Foreword.

There is another group who are almost done with church, but not "done" with Jesus.[3] They, like Mark, are looking for something that will give life to their faith, excite their imagination, propel them on to the road following Jesus. If they don't find it, the risk is they might leave the church altogether. When they go, they will quietly exit through the back door and seek their own rhythms of faith. If this sounds uncomfortably familiar, then this book is for you.

When Mark told me of his departure from organized religion, I wish I knew then what I know now. In many ways, his story was almost my story. This book is the narrative I would now tell him, and the narrative I would share with anyone who

---

3 Ibid., 17.

loves Jesus and has a gnawing feeling there must be more to their faith than the few hours they spend a week within the walls of the church building.

Over decades, even centuries, the church has morphed into a destination, a building, an event, where people come to "find God." While the gathering of God's people to sing, observe the sacraments, and receive teaching from the Scriptures is a necessary and helpful rhythm to our faith, the church has forgotten her primary purpose of being a *sending* agent to equip her people to announce the kingdom of God to the world. The story of God throughout Scripture is the story of a missional God who then sends us on mission. Yes, we are meant to be a *gathered* people at times, but we also find our Jesus identity in being a *scattered* people, announcing the reign of God in King Jesus. We must reclaim our missional identity, partnering with God in taking the gospel to the streets where we live. The gathered church equips us to carry out that calling and identity.

Faith, Christianity, following Jesus, is all about living life out loud.

Introduction:
Everybody Plays

When I was young, baseball was like church in my family. My grandfather (Papa) played some semi-professional ball, and one of my dad's good friends was a professional pitcher for a time. As I started playing in structured baseball leagues I found myself on the mound, pitching throughout my illustrious little-league and school career. Dad and Papa looked on with pride when they came to watch me pitch in weekend games, excited that I might have baseball in my blood. I remember my dad's friend showing me how to throw a curve ball, which was rarely seen in little league. With his help, I actually had some "stuff" to throw, and so I gained the position of starting pitcher for the team.

In addition to throwing a ball, I could run pretty fast, so I tried out for the track team and made a couple of sprint relay teams. We temporarily, but excitedly, held some state records. Surely, success in baseball and track *must* have meant I could play any sport, so I eventually went out for football. A lot of my friends were first-string players and had been urging me to come to try-outs every year, but I had been hesitant. I remember being dragged to the gym to line up and sign my name on the interest sheet.

When I showed up that day after classes, the coaches seemed pretty happy. They knew I was on the track team, and so they saw me as some kind of receiver. If they could just get me the ball, I could hopefully turn on the speed. However, there was something about getting hit fifteen seconds after catching the ball which kept me from being overly enthusiastic about playing. The idea of hitting others as hard as I could, and getting hit in return, prevented me from being "all in" with football. I did make the team, but most of the time I found myself warming the bench as a second-string receiver.

This didn't make me totally unhappy, because, after all, I was part of the team! I had a uniform, I was a member, I had devoured the playbook, and I got to hang out with the whole team, including the starters. The quarterback and running backs were my friends, and we'd hang out together after school or on weekends, but when it came to game time, I cheered them on while they ran the plays. I would watch them run a play, and I'd know exactly what it was because I had memorized it from the playbook we all possessed. In some ways it felt like I was playing football, but I really wasn't: I was watching others run the plays.

Then that game night came when I heard six-foot six-inch Coach Ferriter bellow out those words. Up and down the sidelines the echo came, *"Everybody plays!"* All of a sudden the assistant coaches started replacing first-string players on the field with us second-stringers. In a moment I heard, "Smith, you're in," from my receivers coach. Now *we* were running the plays. To be honest, the whole thing caught me by surprise, but our team was several touchdowns ahead, and the coach wanted everybody to have the experience of being on the field. We were not as good, nor as smooth at running the plays as the first-string, but we could run them all the same. For the few remaining games of the season I waited for those two words toward the end of every game: "*Everybody plays.*" I found joy, meaning and excitement in running the plays I had memorized. The view from being on the field was exhilarating and I loved it. I lost my fear of being hit and found myself immersed in the rhythms of the game.

With every hit on the field I was learning what it meant to actually play the game, and I found myself drawn to being more than just a member of the team. I remember one game when we ran a play out of our playbook—a "52 Squirrel." After catching the ball, then running about ten yards, I received one of the hardest hits I've ever experienced, as two guys twice my size launched me off my feet, and off the field, onto my own sidelines. I remember getting up, seeing the coaches smiling, and then patting me on the pads with an encouragement of, "Way to go, Smith!" It was painful, but it was one of the best memories of my childhood. I had run the play, received some jolts, and now had gained an identity as a football player.

Ironically, I now felt some disappointment when the horn sounded each night to end the game. At the end of the season I found myself wishing I had given all of myself to football earlier on. It was exhilarating! The bench had become boring; the field was where the excitement was.

In the church we often make the mistake of thinking there is a first-string and second-string team. We hire a gifted teaching pastor, a talented worship leader, a dynamic children's pastor, and other great staff, then sit back on the bench (in the pew), and watch them run the plays. We think we're not equipped or trained enough to actually be in the game, so we hire professionals who are trained to be the first-string players. Every once in a while the second-string is asked to participate, but it's usually to fulfill the plans and vision of the first-string. This system unintentionally creates two groups in the church: those who sit on the bench and those who run the plays. This is most likely what caused my friend Mark, introduced to you in the Preface, to leave the church in search of a more meaningful faith.

This is also where I lived for twenty-two years in ministry. No, not on the bench—I was a first-stringer. I was leading worship, teaching, and serving on executive leadership teams in mid to larger-sized churches. I would carefully craft worship experiences each week to fit perfectly with the sermon. I would often help run outreach programs designed to invite people to our church building. I was an expert in technology and concert production, so I could make a Sunday stage emotionally moving for those in attendance. All the lights matched the backgrounds, the band was rehearsed, the flow from one element of the service to the next was skillfully timed.

None of those things were necessarily bad in themselves, and I don't recall consciously having a wrong intention behind them, but what I eventually realized was that I was actually teaching people an incomplete and unsatisfying rhythm of religion. I was supporting the notion that Christian faith was defined by church attendance, giving, and simply gaining more knowledge about God, whether that be through sermons, Bible studies, or other programs. I was reinforcing the belief that *ministry happened primarily at the church building.* My realizations were confirmed as I met more and more people who were bored with their faith, just as Mark was. I kept trying to do more and more tweaking to the Sunday stage experience but found myself in competition against more meaningful things in people's lives: camping with family, attending a football game, eating with neighbors, or just hiking our Colorado mountains. They wanted more of Jesus and their faith than a weekend event, and silently I found myself wanting the same thing. The weekly rhythm of preparing an event at the church building wasn't only empty in terms of my work life, it left me wanting more in my own spiritual life as well. I wanted to know the Jesus of the Scriptures, not just the Jesus of the Sunday monologue. The Jesus I read and heard about on Sundays seemed to call for a bigger and louder life than I was experiencing by simply producing Sunday events. It wasn't that the worship service was bad; I just knew there was more. Following Jesus went far beyond what we were asking of church members. And so I set off on a journey, one that had been calling my name for many years. I'd heard it whispering but had ignored its call.

Outside of my job at church I often found myself engaged with stories that would never be talked about in a Sunday service. These were stories of extreme brokenness, messy situations, with people who would never consider darkening the door of a church building. We had homeless teens living with us, single moms, foster kids. We found ourselves in the middle of broken marriages.

My life inside the church felt antiseptic, clean, and well-kept. The other part of my life with people's circumstances outside the church walls looked less organized, not "fine," and was often painful. It felt like two disconnected lives trying to follow the same Jesus. The time came when I had to face up to how God was calling me. I had to accept it was going to require courage, some level of risk, and would actually cost me something. The reality I learned might shatter my identity as a pastor, might cost me my job, and might involve some major life choices. But I had to face it if I was going to step onto the field and into the game.

In the kingdom there is no bench: *everybody plays.* The kingdom is set up as one playing field, and we're all on that field together, running the plays of the mission of God. Our weekly Christian rhythms, often inadvertently taught and supported by many churches, can actually keep us *out* of the game, and instead encourage us to support the primary team on the field. We find ourselves in the locker room weekly, talking about *how* to run the plays and *why* we run the plays, but we don't know with *whom* or *where* we run the plays. We leave Sunday church services with a "thank you for being here," then make our way through the parking lot with no sense of mission for the week ahead. We just spent some time on the bench, and in some ways we feel like we're part of the team, but if that is the extent of our game-time, it is tragically deficient.

That is what I hope to rectify in this book. I want to reveal some of the things I've learned in finding an exciting life following Jesus, living a louder life for the kingdom. They were paradigm shifts for me, and I believe they will be for you as well. These shifts in thinking are a doorway to allow God's desired mission to invade our life, our priorities, and our imagination. I want you to have the experience I had when the coach put me on the field and I discovered an exhilarating experience of actually being in the game. I'm hoping the stories and examples in this book will show you that you are not a second-stringer. You are called to be on the field and joining Jesus outside the walls of the church, redeeming the world and restoring people's lives. You won't believe what it feels like to actually run with the ball! Yes, it can be a scary thing to step on the field and play, rather than watch and listen to others talk about it. And yes, you might actually get hit once in a while. I promise you, though, the life out loud that follows Jesus is found in the willingness to ask some daring questions about your own life. Once you get over the fear of being hit, you come to relish the truth that all of us—every pastor, every church leader, every person in the pew, me, you, *everybody*—plays.

In Colorado Springs we live right next to the Rocky Mountains. Our community is nestled up against what we call, "The Front Range." These are the foothills that are visible to us *before* we can even see the grand snowcapped peaks of the Rockies. Those of us who have driven into the foothills know that, with the exception of Pikes Peak, the Rockies are hidden just a short ten to fifteen-minute drive away. Anyone who has not made the drive up Highway 24 might ask, "Where are the numerous great peaks of the Rockies I see in pictures and postcards?" They are there, but they are *just out of sight.*

I found my needed rhythms of following Jesus living just out of sight of my weekly church experience. The potential for a purposeful faith was always there, but I couldn't see a meaningful path of following Jesus past the pressures to keep the institution afloat. Christianity was defined by everything I did in church meetings and events, but I discovered this was just a partial expression of my faith. And so, I asked my own daring questions, which led to some loud, radical changes in my life.

I resigned from my position at a church, with its very comfortable salary and situation, and instead, sought a way to tangibly live out the gospel in our city. My wife, Kitty, and I opened a large coffee shop where we could interact with all facets of community in Colorado Springs. We launched a small, strange band of people as a faith community, which meets around a table, eating, talking about the Scriptures, praying, and asking how we can live out our faith with others. We got involved with Forge America, a tribe that speaks the language of our heart, and began training others on missional practices in life. Eventually, I also found my way back into a larger church environment, but instead of reconstructing the same rhythms I had left behind, I began working with a leadership team, joining them to expand the kingdom of God by equipping and launching people out into their city and neighborhoods, outside the walls of the building.

Just one loud, life-altering question, led to some really scary steps onto the field, and God opened up an amazing world of joining him in mission. It's the question I dare you to ask as well: "Jesus, how and where can I best follow you?" The experiences I share in this book, some from my own life, some from others, now shape me as a Christ-follower and leave me in wonder of how God works through me and through others. If you ask and answer this same question, I am confident you will be amazed at how he also works through you.

These paradigms of how to live were just one perspective away, just past the foothills, always in the playbook, but not always being played out in my life. When I look back, I can't believe I missed them. I invite you into a short glimpse of the life out loud that I now see, the world I believe God invites you into as well. Let him and his mission invade your imagination and you won't believe where he leads.

One of my favorite movies has always been *The Wizard of Oz.* [4] You may remember the beginning of the movie is filmed in black and white. This lack of color illustrates the American

---

4 *The Wizard of Oz*, directed by Victor Fleming, Metro-Goldwyn-Mayer, 1939, film.

mid-west during the depression and the dust storms of Kansas. When Dorothy falls asleep she begins to have a dream of her house being caught up in a tornado and is tossed about violently. When the house finally comes to rest, she goes to the door and opens it. Magically the film goes from black and white to vibrant color. She walks out of her black and white life and is suddenly surrounded by a world in living color.

I want your world to be vibrant, full of living color, full of life. What I truly believe is that it may be just one loud question away, one foot on the field, one drive into the foothills! Would you risk asking the question if it meant a deeply meaningful and exciting life following Jesus? If you could get up every morning knowing exactly how Jesus wants you to live in this crazy world today, outside the church walls, would you tempt some time on the field of play? Would you catch a ball and run a sideline? I'm not asking you to play right this second, but I am asking you to keep reading, all the time considering your own faith life and how you define it. Are you bored or unsatisfied with your faith? Does Christianity feel like a religious hamster wheel? Does the story of God include the things *you* do every day, or are you watching others from the sideline? Could a few daring questions cause major changes in your life? Maybe, but it may just be one small shift of perspective in the places you already live. You may not be called to quit a job or open a business. I truly hope you don't feel called to leave the church like many are doing today. We are all called to follow Jesus in our lives.

However, I'm pretty sure he didn't ask us to just follow him to a church building and back home each Sunday. He called us to something *louder*!

Take a chance and read further. Start asking questions like I did and see if God isn't calling you to join him! My guess is, if you listen closely, you'll hear…"Everybody plays."

I'm Only Human

As I pulled out of the Costco parking lot I saw a young woman huddled next to the stop sign across the lane. She was noticeably sobbing and holding a white cardboard sign in her lap. I had been on a shopping trip for our coffee shop, Third Space Coffee, and like everyone else, was in a hurry to get back to my business and on with my very full day. Waiting my turn to go through the intersection, I saw four cars pass her by and go on their way. This wasn't abnormal, though. Beggars and people in trouble are passed by all the time. "I live my life, you live your life" is often the unspoken mantra of our society.

Something told me I had to stop and talk to her. I pulled into a parking spot and walked over to ask her what was wrong. Looking at me with an emotionally worn face, Ashley explained she was begging for gas money so she could leave her abusive husband and travel back to Texas. "I'm just not very good at begging," she sobbed. She looked at me and said,

"I know my marriage is another failure and I've screwed up my life, but I guess I'm only human."

I knew that a group of women from our faith community were meeting in our shop for a Bible study, so I asked Ashley to follow me back to Third Space. When we arrived, I led her over to where they were meeting, and at once, this group embraced her, closed their Bibles and began to love her. They reserved a hotel room for the drive halfway to Texas, gave her some pocket money, and we made a care package of sandwiches and snacks for her trip. They prayed with her and then she left with tears in her eyes, partly from the pain in her life, partly from the love she had been shown by others. That group of women could have reopened their Bibles and shown Ashley all the verses that didn't seem to line up with her life. They easily could have turned to Ephesians 5 and talked of how a biblical marriage worked, or multiple passages about unity and loving each other, but they chose to take the message of Jesus and the example of his life and simply love another person, without judgment or inspection of their sin. At that moment, the message of the Scriptures, of loving God and loving your neighbor, needed to become a reality, and so the Bibles were closed and love became more than knowledge: it became a verb.

I still to this day don't know if Ashley was a Christ-follower or not, but I knew in that instant she was, like me, another creation of God, desperately needing to be seen. That group of women acknowledged and communicated this with their actions. Ashley's comment about her failures and being "only human" stuck with me. We all lean on that phrase when we need it, when life gives us a gut punch, when we fail or fall. That day, Ashley wasn't feeling on top of life. She was only human.

"I'm only human" is one of the clarifying clichés of our culture, enabling us to justify the mistakes, missteps and failings of our lives. It's the comeback that cannot be trumped. "I'm only human" is an equalizing statement, which elicits grace, and demands empathy. Sometimes it's the phrase of surrender to the circumstances we find ourselves drowning in. When we can't fix it and save face, being only human is the next best result.

This secular statement ironically almost acknowledges Genesis 3, known as "the Fall," in which sin entered humanity through the disobedience of Adam and Eve. God told Adam and Eve they could eat of any tree in the garden, but they must not eat of the tree of knowledge of good and evil.[5] They disobeyed God and brought sin into the world, seeking to satisfy their cravings and desires. As those who live in the lineage of this story, we carry these same cravings, and so we live in the tension of seeking moral character while also harboring and hosting the desires born from Adam and Eve choosing the fruit of the tree.

We believe, as Christian people, that this parasite of sin is carried in all humanity. We see the brokenness of the world and we can attribute it to this story of our beginnings. We encounter death, hatred, violence, and evil in the world and look

---

5 Genesis 2:17.

back to the garden as the birthplace of sin. In our own failures, we can acknowledge this unchosen lineage, owning it in the phrase, "I'm only human."

You may see Genesis 3 as a factual and historical account of humankind's fall into sin, or you may see the Garden story as a metaphor, illustrating that sin invaded the perfection of creation. Either way, while the statement "I'm only human" is certainly true, it can present us with problems in the way we view ourselves, the way we view our relationship with God, and maybe more importantly, the way we view others.

The Greatest Identity

Consider for a moment a new perspective: that humanity is not a deficit, not a failure or a thing to overcome. Maybe it's not a hill to climb throughout your life, where each stumble and poor decision is pacified with the statement, "I'm only human." What if being human was the greatest identity we could hope to carry? What if it was a calling, a gift, an incredible invitation from the Creator to be like-minded, like-spirited, and in partnership with him? I would suggest that being human is perhaps the greatest gift offered from our Creator as it invites us to be a mirror-image of his heart and his love for humanity and creation. Perhaps being human gives us this sacred identity and permission to speak into the reconciliation and redemption of his created world. It can also become our call to others, that through the redemption of Jesus Christ they can rise above the entrapment of sin to live into this great gift and identity.

Dirt

Early in the timeline of the Bible, Genesis 2 describes God's creation of man and woman. It poetically presents God's desire to create something special. You might think such a creation would require a special material or substance, but no, God chooses dirt. Genesis tells us, "then the Lord God formed the man of dust from the ground and breathed into his nostrils the breath of life, and the man became a living creature" (Genesis 2:7 ESV). In Hebrew, "breath of life" is the word *Ruach,* and is considered equivalent to the word *Spirit.*[6]

Genesis 2:7 presents this picture of God breathing his Spirit into dust to create mankind. Using the same element we endlessly clean from our homes, God not only creates life, but life created to resemble him. Dirt becomes the basic building block of humanity, and then we, this dust of the ground, hosting God's breath of Spirit, are made in his likeness and image, the *imago Dei*, the image of God.

This invites a whole new way to look at the phrase, "I'm only human." Being *only* human focuses on the dirt, and fails to see the breath of God within ourselves, and within others. Seeing ourselves as *only* human is at odds with our identity as an image of God, our Creator. Being *only* human misses the incredible honor of being fashioned into the likeness of the One doing the creating. We can forget that God himself wants us as images of him. He could have created anything, but he

---

6 D. Tasker, "Ruach Elohim: The Holy Spirit in the Old Testament," *Ministry: International Journal for Pastors*, 85, 1, (2013), 16–19.

chose to create woman and man in his image, *imago Dei*.

I understand the tension in this perspective. Many days in my own life have felt dustier than others. I've had whole seasons of wading through mud and grime, sometimes my fault, sometimes at the hands of others. In those times, it's very hard to feel like an image of God. We can be weighed down by the dirt we carry, our very foundational building block, and the identity of dust seemingly rises to the top, overshadowing our identity as carriers of his breath. Our vision might be clouded by the storm of dust in our life, yet still we carry this image of the Creator, even in the midst of the storm.

We live in a world that often sees our dirt before our *imago Dei*, and so we sometimes pay more attention to sweeping away the dirt in our life than living into the image we've been given in that dust. There are times when the dirt actually shapes us more into an image of God, but it can be hard to see in the midst of the dust storm.

James, the brother of Jesus, writes in his letter which ended up in the Bible:

> Consider it a sheer gift, friends, when tests and challenges come at you from all sides. You know that under pressure, your faith-life is forced into the open and shows its true colors. So don't try to get out of anything prematurely. Let it do its work so you become mature and well-developed, not deficient in any way.
>
> JAMES 1:2–4 (MSG)

At times the dusty parts of life, and the dust within us, will help force the *imago Dei* into the open. Our trials can build us up, make us look more like our Creator, if we strive for the image of his Spirit, rather than the original building block of dirt.

Sometimes, life can seem like a pendulum, swinging back and forth between these two images…dirt and God's breath. This is the reality of living with sin within us and in a world that is ruled by that sin. We are exiles in a land that is not our home, a world that falls short of heaven. No one is just a basic building block of dirt, even though it sometimes feels like it. God's breath was joined with dirt, he called it good, and created us all. We, everyone, are the *imago Dei*.

The Primary Truth

As Jesus people we walk with the understanding that there is tension in this life. We constantly strive for the perfection God designed in Genesis 1 and 2, but often fall and stumble into the story our ancestors wrote in Genesis 3.

Once we realize we carry this image of God in our life, it is easier to see our fellow sojourners in the world who carry this image as well. Sure, some have not yet put their faith in Jesus Christ as we would hope, but we must appreciate that Genesis 1 was the precursor to a relationship with God, even for Adam and Eve. He created them in his image first. My friend Deb Hirsch makes the point that how we view others greatly affects our approach to them. If we see others first in their fallenness, their sinful behavior, or the way they live, then we are focusing on what she calls the "secondary truth" about them. The primary truth about them is also the primary truth about us: they, and we, are an *imago Dei*, an image of God.[7] "After all," Deb will often proclaim, "Genesis 1 came before Genesis 3."

When we come to this realization, then our view of other human beings, and humanity as a whole, radically changes. You may know someone who has a different belief system, they may have a different sexual orientation, or they may have behaviors that are complicating their life, which may, in practice, feel uncomfortable to your theology. But when we understand that all of us are living a journey as God's image, broken by the story of Genesis 3, yet still seeking identity as his creation, then we can appreciate a person for who they are, rather than focusing on their behaviors or differing belief system. What becomes painfully obvious is that all of humanity is on a journey of discovering their identity. As Christians, we often try to draw clean lines that separate behavior and belief, but we know personally that we still grapple with a life between Genesis 1 and 3. We find our own lives leaning hard back to the breath of God, wanting to leave a life identified by sin. We want our identity to be in Jesus, not the dirt that feels absent of God's breath. For those of us who follow Jesus, we have found the forgiveness of our sin in the work of the cross and the resurrection. Yet even in this redemptive state we often still feel the effects of dirt.

Others we meet may still be seeking identity and possibly

7 Alan and Debra Hirsch, *Untamed* (Grand Rapids: Baker Books, 2010), 194–195.

faith; they sometimes seem stuck in the dirt...scratching through life issues, addictions, relationships, success, or other identity labels. They may just be looking for that breath of God, which unknowingly already exists within them. They may have tremendous dirt under their fingernails of life, but they are still fellow images, seeking their true identity. It's as if God's breath is there but needs to be activated through relationship with Jesus and the redemption he offers. Just as we have found hope in the cross of Jesus, bringing us home to our true identity as God's children, others are searching and can find that identity as well. It's theirs to claim, theirs to activate from the dirt of the ground. It's innate within them, born into them as creations of God. Often, when I see co-creations of God living in ways absent of his presence, I see someone searching for breath. Though their life choices may look very different from mine, they are no less human than me, made from the same dust, searching for that completed resuscitation of God's breath in their life, a completed identity.

As Christians, we have the privilege of telling others and the world, "No, you are not just dirt; you are an image of the one who created you." Part of the mission of God (the *missio Dei*) is for his followers to show the world that they are not just enlivened dust trapped in a material being, but they are made by a commingling of the dust of the earth (which God called good in Genesis 1) and the *Ruach* breath of God's spirit breathed into us—*all* of us. As we come in contact with others in the places we live, work, and play, having this framework and understanding of our beginnings will allow us to see people differently. We're not threatened, because *essentially* we're the same: same dirt, same issues, just different points of the journey. Because of this, we can find our commonality and our love for our neighbor. We are the same dirt and same breath of God.

Flesh

In the Gospels, Jesus shows us how to live as carriers and announcers of the kingdom of God. Many times, Christians look at the Gospels, and the rest of the Bible, and create a rule book, reducing the teachings and encounters of Scripture to propositional statements and bullet points. We can create a checklist of sorts, which delineates life with God into things that are right and other things that are wrong. We want the Bible to tell us exactly what to do in a messy world. So we mistakenly take parables, songs, poetry, and teachings, and create an instruction manual to live by, rather than seeing the God-inspired Scriptures as a tension-filled story of God with flesh on, who came to announce and show us what the kingdom of God looks like.

Author Skye Jethani points out,

> His plan to restore creation was not to send a list of rules and rituals to follow (LIFE UNDER GOD), nor was it the implementation of useful principles (LIFE OVER GOD). He did not send a genie to grant us our desires (LIFE FROM GOD), nor did he give us a task to accomplish (LIFE FOR GOD). Instead God himself came to be

with us—to walk with us once again as he had
done in Eden in the beginning. Jesus entered into
our dark existence to share our broken world
and to illuminate a different way forward.[8]

There's a word that has become a big part of my vocabulary in this new way of life following Jesus. It's a concept called the Incarnation. Without getting stuck in theological discussion here, the Incarnation is the concept of Jesus being human while also being God. The term *Incarnation* literally means "to take on flesh."

We see Jesus' incarnation described in the Gospel of John:

In the beginning was the Word, and the Word
was with God, and the Word was God. He was
with God in the beginning. Through him all
things were made; without him nothing was
made that has been made. In him was life,
and that life was the light of all mankind[...]
The Word *became flesh* and made his dwelling
among us. We have seen his glory, the glory
of the one and only Son, who came from the
Father, full of grace and truth.

JOHN 1:1–4,14 (italics mine)

You can see this concept of Incarnation in the words I italicized, where Jesus, the Word, becomes flesh and lives, walks,

8 Skye Jethani, *With: Reimagining the Way You Relate to God* (Nashville, TN: Thomas Nelson, 2011), 100.

and works among us. This living among us is documented in the Gospels, the accounts of Jesus' life on Earth. Ultimately this whole study of God becoming flesh among us creates this doctrine, or belief, referred to as the Incarnation. Jesus becomes the perfect in-flesh example of the joining of God's breath with dust, walking amongst us.

I love the way Eugene Peterson translates this incarnation verse in the Gospel of John, "The Word became flesh and blood, and moved into the neighborhood" (John 1:14 MSG). Thinking of Jesus moving into my neighborhood helps me compose a visual of God with skin on. What might it look like if Jesus was my actual neighbor? What would he be like? What might we talk about? Would the whole neighborhood become more religious all of a sudden, if Jesus moved in?

In the Gospels, we see Jesus engaging in the neighborhoods he walks in. We can read the accounts of him healing and teaching people about the kingdom of God. We see him love children, prostitutes, the poor, and the lame. We see him showing compassion on those who are living dusty lives, somewhere between dirt and the breath of God. This incarnational life of Jesus, where God and man dwell amongst other *imago Dei,* is the foundational subject matter of the Gospels and also becomes the foundational model for the way we live as Jesus people.

When we read the Bible, we sometimes miss the rhythms and ways in which Jesus announces the kingdom. We miss the encounters he intentionally has with those who are living life searching for their own meaning, sometimes scratching through the dirt of sin or brokenness. Jesus sees them in their Genesis 1 identity first, as images of the Father, lifting their heads above the dirt and breathing life into them again.[9] For those who define people by their behavior and beliefs, usually the Pharisees and Sadducees, Jesus has critical feedback at best. At worst he calls them vipers and serpents.[10]

Broken, sinful lives did not separate people from Jesus. Rather, their circumstances often brought them closer to him. Those the religious system of the day pushed to the side were invited closer to Jesus. His message was simple: Genesis 1 comes before Genesis 3.

Little Christs

You may think, as someone who is "only human," that it would be impossible to live out an identity or concept like the Incarnation. I would propose to you that we are *meant* to live incarnationally. Now, before you call me a heretic for suggesting we are all gods "in the flesh," I am not proposing we are God. But I would share the thinking of author C.S. Lewis, who writes:

> Now the whole offer which Christianity makes is this: that we can, if we let God have His way, come to share in the life of Christ. If we do, we shall then be sharing a life which was begotten,

---

9 For examples, see John 8:1–11; John 4:4–42; Mark 1:40–45; John 9:1–12.
10 Matthew 23:33.

not made, which always existed and always will exist. Christ is the Son of God. If we share in this kind of life we also shall be sons of God. We shall love the Father as He does and the Holy Ghost will arise in us. He came to this world and became a man in order to spread to other men the kind of life He has—by what I call "good infection." Every Christian is to become a little Christ. The whole purpose of becoming a Christian is simply nothing else.[11]

Lewis' point, and mine, is that we carry the essence of incarnation when we live as Christ lived. When our rhythm is in concert with the Holy Spirit and the desires of God's will, then we can live a life that might be termed "only human" at times but is radically redeemed and restored by Jesus Christ. What Jesus has done for us becomes the lens through which we see others. As a result, we live as examples of his grace by demonstrating that grace to others. We give power to the grace in our own life when we, as little Christs, live intentionally with others and show them what this grace tangibly looks like. This may seem like a pretty big identity to carry. For those who see themselves as "only human," it is. But for those who see themselves first as people who are breath carriers of God's Spirit, those redeemed by the grace of God, it is an identity to live into, and also a lens through which to view others. It's like the glasses we wear through life, where our own restored, grace-filled identity in

11 C.S. Lewis, *Mere Christianity* (New York: HarperOne, 1952), 177.

Jesus brings into focus the way we see and live with others.

In his memorable book *The Ragamuffin Gospel,* Brennan Manning tells of how Jesus lived out his grace with others:

> Jesus sat down at the table with anyone who wanted to be present, including those who were banished from decent homes. In sharing of a meal they received consideration instead of expected condemnation. A merciful acquittal instead of a hasty verdict of guilty. Amazing grace instead of universal disgrace. Here is a very practical demonstration of the law of grace—a new chance at life.[12]

As our actions and life replicate the life of Jesus, we can become in a sense, as Lewis suggests, "little Christs." We show the redeemed life of an image of God, in whom we have found not only salvation through the cross, but a way of living incarnationally with others, with the presence of God in our life and actions. As Jesus lived incarnationally amongst us, we represent his incarnational presence as he lives through us. We can become the carriers of his breath and examples of his grace.

Putting Our Flesh On

If *imago Dei* is our identity, not something we can achieve, but something given to us, then living incarnationally is the

---

12 Brennan Manning, *The Ragamuffin Gospel* (Oregon: Multnomah Publishers, Inc: Sisters, 1990), 29.

way we put that identity in motion. *Imago Dei* is who we are; incarnational living is what we do to carry that identity into the world.

Jesus gives us a great picture of this in his encounter with a Samaritan woman. This passage of Scripture found in John 4, often named "The woman at the well," is preached from pulpits around the world, usually supporting points and propositions regarding our worship of God. It also offers a helpful model of living incarnationally. As twenty-first-century readers, we often miss the outrageous nature of this story. Being a Jewish rabbi and sitting with a Samaritan woman, Jesus most certainly brought on gasps and murmurs. Simply engaging in conversation with not only a woman but also a stranger raised one point of social order, but for a Jew to associate with a Samaritan took this encounter to a new level of scandal. When you add to the story her five husbands, as well as the man she was currently living with, then you realize her journey was fodder for gossip around the town. However, Jesus engages her as an image of God needing new breath in her life. Her shame is washed with Living Water—Jesus himself. It's as if Jesus refuses to let her live in an, "I'm only human" state. To him, she is much more than her behavior, more than dirt.

Potential Energy

The concept of incarnational living reminds me of a school lesson that has always stuck with me. I had a science teacher in middle school who was very good at illustrating the laws of physics and nature to us. He used a certain example to teach us about a concept called *potential energy*. This concept defines materials or elements that have latent energy stored in them but have yet to produce that energy, until something else is added to it. For example, let's take a can of gasoline, possibly sitting next to the lawnmower in your garage or shed. That can of gas has potential energy in it, explosive energy actually. I sleep pretty well at night, even though I have several of these cans of gas and fuel distributed amongst our shed and garage. I'm not concerned they will explode, knowing that contained in the can by itself, the gasoline will act like a liquid and just sit there. It smells like gasoline, it chemically meets all the qualifications of gasoline, and is potentially dangerous. However, its identity as gasoline, its reason for existence, is only made complete when a spark or fire is added to it. Exploding is its pure and unarguable destiny—an activation of its identity.

Similarly, all people carry the identity of *imago Dei*, but not everyone fully lives into this. It requires following Jesus into what might feel like uncomfortable places, places that don't always feel safe. Jesus was the ultimate *imago Dei* in the Incarnation: God and man together as Christ. But Genesis 1 tells us that every person was made in God's image in this act of breathing into dust. So yes, your fellow Christ-follower is *imago Dei*, but so is your neighbor, co-worker and family member, even though they don't yet identify with Jesus, or maybe live counter to what you interpret as biblical. All carry the identity of *imago Dei*, whether they live into that identity or not.

It's an issue of potential energy that has yet to be put in motion. A relationship with Jesus and the presence of God in our life is the fire that will activate and cause our identity to explode. This is exactly what happened to the woman at the well: the offer of Living Water, Jesus, sent her frantically running through her village to tell of the Messiah who had come and shown her grace.[13] Until a person's given identity as *imago Dei* is activated by the presence of God, they are living as potential incarnational energy. The incarnational life of the Christ-follower explodes, as the fire of the Holy Spirit is present in their life through the grace of God.

Living daily as a little Christ, incarnationally, isn't defined by weekly church attendance. Simply attending church services and programs will likely never result in the explosion of our potential energy, never activate a fully incarnational life. Church events, sermons, and other activities are often designed to put more gas in the can, more knowledge in our head. Many people are absolutely ready to explode with all the knowledge and energy stored up in them from years of sitting in pews. Acquiring knowledge, having potential energy, is not a bad thing, but if it lies dormant, just a can of gas, then the created identity is never realized.

Instead, our identity as Christ-followers is driven externally, like an explosion. And like an explosion, it becomes life out loud. It is more about how others are affected by our identity as *imago Dei* than how we personally are affected by

13 John 4:28–42.

worship services. In my experience, once we start living an incarnational presence amongst others, we see amazing things start to happen: we see the power of God in our life. Stories of being used by God to activate others' identities become a common occurrence. We see miracles happen as God uses us to display his power to other people. Our highlight reels of living for Jesus become populated almost daily, instead of being rare occurrences. The more we live an externally focused, incarnational lifestyle, the more we witness the explosive nature of joining our given identity of God's image and the activating result of incarnational living. Sometimes the journey with others will be long-term and deep; sometimes you'll simply feel led to stop for a woman crying at a stop sign. You may have the opportunity to sit at a well with someone and show value to them first as a fellow image of God; you may possibly be given the opportunity to talk about Living Water. But whatever the circumstance, our first response is not to engage people through the lens of religious rules or "right living," but to first see them as created in God's image, just like you and me.

When we start practicing the activities of living as God's image to others, then our knowledge is exploded into the places we live, work, and play. Explosion stories start happening all around us. Faith and following Jesus become an adventure, and the phrase "I'm only human" fades into the background, not only for us, but for those we come in contact with.

ONE LOUDER STEP

Identify a person or group with a differing lifestyle or belief system and begin to visualize them as fellow *imago Dei* (images of God) first. See the person, not the differences. Make an effort to get to know them.

2

A Better Great Commission?

As we came over the hill in two jeeps and a Land Rover, we saw the valley sitting next to the Yangtze river and a small village of stone houses huddled together. Out in the valley next to the river were twenty or so vibrantly colored tents with flags flying from the top. There were horses and riders, dressed from head to toe with colorful garments, braids of red, yellow, and purple cloth woven in the manes and tails of the horses. It felt as if we had gone through a time machine and were driving right into the Tibetan culture of 400 years earlier. Our Tibetan hosts saw us coming over the ridge and began scurrying to gather together in a ritual welcome. Horses rode out to meet our jeeps and lead us in. As we approached the crowd, they began playing drums and music as they danced and sang for us. The horses and riders began a traditional race up and down the field. We couldn't tell who was winning or what was going on, so we just followed the crowd and cheered whenever they did. That night, we sat in tents eating yak jerky and fruit. Some of us found our way out to the banks of the Yangtze river, the longest river in Asia and third longest in the world. We lay back on the banks, staring up at a million stars, a cigar in one hand and a Chinese beer in the other. My world as a worship pastor in Arkansas was a distant memory, overtaken by the intoxication of the culture in which I found myself.

We spent the next three weeks in various Tibetan and Chinese contexts, exploring the countryside and meeting people, all in the hope of starting a rug factory in which missionaries could live and work side by side with the Tibetan nationals. Tibet stole my heart, along with its neighboring parent-state, China. The experience of crossing over from my culture to theirs opened my eyes to the world and, more importantly, what God was doing in it. It was my first foray into what the church calls "missions." The box, back in Arkansas, where I kept God and my theology, became much bigger—huge in fact! I had to join in and be part of this bigger world. God had captured my imagination with the idea of living on mission for the kingdom. Little did I know he would further expand my concept of missions later in life.

Missions Introductions

Well before my trip to Tibet, I was baptized in a Southern Baptist church in Arkansas at the age of twenty-two, and immediately came in contact with the word "missions." I quickly learned about something called the Lottie Moon Christmas Offering. Lottie Moon had been a missionary to China for over forty years, and this organization honored her legacy by continuing to make the gospel known in China and around the world. This particular church saw the organization of Lottie Moon as a primary way to support "missions" around the globe, and so church members were challenged to give financially and reach a monetary goal to give Lottie Moon each year.

Like many others, this church defined "mission" as cross-cultural (usually defined as overseas) work, in which the gospel is shared either with those who have no Bible in their native language or with those who have an apparent lack of Christian presence in their culture. And so, I learned that a missionary was someone who primarily went overseas to share the gospel with people who didn't know it. In this church culture there was also an unspoken belief that some were called to missions work, and some were called to support their efforts. Overseas missionaries had a special calling to be "out there" doing the work of the gospel. For the rest of us, our call was to financially and prayerfully support them. And so, unintentionally, I learned early on that missions work was something that was done overseas by other supernaturally called people, and I simply cheered them on. At this point in my life as a new believer, I had a seat on the bench, rooting for the team on the field.

The source and genesis of missions work around the world comes from a good place: direct instructions from Jesus. There is a world that needs to hear the good news of Jesus, and the church is given the mission to spread that news.

In the final chapter of the Gospel of Matthew Jesus says:

> "All authority in heaven and on earth has been given to me. Therefore go and make disciples of all nations, baptizing them in the name of the Father and of the Son and of the Holy Spirit, and teaching them to obey everything I have commanded you. And surely I am with you always, to the very end of the age."
>
> MATTHEW 28:18–20

This piece of Scripture has been adopted by the church at large and given the title, "The Great Commission." For hundreds of years, this passage has been imperative in taking the message of Jesus all over the world: it's very clear, it gives us a mission to do, and it was given by Jesus himself. Jesus told us to go, and so we go. Well, not all of us, but we do send people to go as our representatives. And so the church, as an institution, "goes" around the world and carries out this command of Jesus. However, not all Jesus' disciples see themselves as the recipients of this instruction. It is often left for those with a higher calling, those we call "missionaries."

Over its life as an institution, the church has developed a way of living out The Great Commission in a manner that lets most of us off the hook. When we read Jesus' instruction to "Go," we read it organizationally, as a large group. We outsource mission, checking it off our list of things to do, as long as we are supporting someone or some organization to carry the gospel cross-culturally.

Each of the churches I was on staff with over my first twenty-two years of ministry had the same structure to support missions: there was a Missions Pastor, a missions budget, and an organizational team of laity who made decisions about financial support to missionaries, in concert with church leadership. It was the job of these good people to steer resources and energy toward missions work appropriate for the calling of The Great Commission. Most of the time, this looked like funding a stable of missionaries that lined up with the church's goals, vision, and theology. Sometimes it meant giving to efforts like Lottie Moon, or perhaps contributing to short-term mission trips (like my trip to Tibet), usually overseas. Each year, we would gather as a church leadership and decide how much of the budget would be allocated to "missions."

I certainly want to acknowledge the good work church organizations achieve through their missions department and committee. And I also appreciate that disciples have been made through overseas missions work over the years and decades. However, by setting up a system where we give the mission of the gospel to a certain, called few (missionaries), and focus what we call "missions" primarily on overseas work, we have unintentionally discipled the everyday person to ignore

Jesus' missional instructions to "Go," in their own context, right where they live, work, and play. Missions work has become, in many cases, something that "other people" do.

We reiterate this message by giving special attention to those who go on short-term mission trips. Those people are often brought up on stage and sent out to their mission field with prayer and applause. However, we rarely pay the same attention to those who love on their local neighborhood. It's not often we allow people to share in a Sunday service about their local missional expression. We don't hear enough about individuals reaching out to the homeless in their own community, or the neighbor next door. We rarely give valuable service time to the vision-casting of creating missionaries out of the average person in the pew, in the everyday places they walk.

Don't get me wrong: all the work and support for missions around the globe is a good and necessary thing. But somehow we've communicated that a mission project is only Great Commission worthy if it comes with a passport. We've tipped the Great Commission to be an "overseas" sending passage, and then in its wake are left those who feel *less called*. Not only is this a really bad interpretation of Scripture, it also breaks the calling of the community as a whole into two parts: those who are called or sent to do the work, and those who stay behind and support them.

The Great Commission passage and sending is for each one of us who follows Jesus. After all, Jesus was talking to his disciples, and so it was a calling for each of them, as well as a calling for his disciples as a whole. We don't elect certain people to become missionaries, short or long term. We are *all* long-term missionaries. We are *all* short-term missionaries. Some are called overseas, some are called to their neighborhood or workplace. In the book of Acts we read of Jesus proclaiming to his disciples, "But you will receive power when the Holy Spirit comes on you; and you will be my witnesses in Jerusalem, and in all Judea and Samaria, and to the ends of the earth" (Acts 1:8). We, the church, are called by Jesus to go and take the gospel message of Jesus to the whole world, overseas, and equally importantly, to our own neighborhood or workplace. If we thought like this, with this framework of missions, I wonder how that might inform the missions budget in the church? Would we separate off a piece of the church's call into a department called Missions, or would we see all the church's work as missions work? Would all the church's budget not be the missions budget?

My point, and question for you is, *how does it feel to be a missionary?*

A Bigger Great Commission

What if we looked at all the missional calls from Jesus and applied them to everyone in the church? Yes, we should expect that some are called overseas for long periods of time where they make disciples, but some are called right where they presently live and work to do the same. Some go on short-term trips overseas to experience cross-cultural work of the kingdom and some do the same right in their own city, in their own country. If everyone *is* a missionary, then we must identify this group in much broader terms. Have you ever seen the "missionary wall" at some churches, where the pictures of those called to announce the gospel cross-culturally are displayed? Well, guess what? Your picture should be up there too!

In another Gospel, Jesus gives another missions statement. I would suggest it equally frames a way of living into mission for each and every one of us, along with the Great Commission in the Gospel of Matthew, and the sending to Jerusalem, Samaria and the ends of the earth, recorded in the book of Acts. It gives us a mission posture from which to then go and do the longer-term relational sharing of the gospel.

We pick up reading in the Gospel of John, when the disciples are gathered after Jesus' crucifixion:

> On the evening of that first day of the week, when the disciples were together, with the doors locked for fear of the Jewish leaders, Jesus came and stood among them and said, "Peace be with you!" After he said this, he showed them his hands and side. The disciples were overjoyed when they saw the Lord. Again Jesus said, "Peace be with you! As the Father has sent me, I am sending you."
>
> JOHN 20:19–21

Notice the last statement from Jesus in this passage. Jesus tells his disciples, "As the Father has sent me, I am sending you." Jesus' message to these disciples, and to us as disciples, is that we are first and foremost a "sent" people. This identity of being "sent" reflects the very nature and heart of God.

Respected missiologist David Bosch insists:

> Mission was understood as being derived from the very nature of God[...]The classical doctrine of the *missio Dei* [mission of God] as God the Father sending the Son, and God the Father and the Son sending the Spirit was expanded to include yet another "movement": Father, Son, and Holy Spirit sending the church into the world[...]Mission is thereby seen as a movement from God to the world; the church is viewed as an instrument for that mission. There is church because there is mission, not vice versa.[14]

Jürgen Moltmann, in a similar vein adds, "It is not the church that has a mission of salvation to fulfill in the world: it is the mission of the Son and the Spirit through the Father that includes the church."[15] In simpler terms, one might say it's not so much that the church has a mission, but that the mission of

---

14 David Bosch, *Transforming Mission: Paradigm Shifts in Theology of Mission* (Maryknoll: Orbis Books, 1991), 389–390.

15 Jürgen Moltmann, *The Church in the Power of the Spirit: A Contribution to Messianic Ecclesiology* (Minneapolis: Fortress Press, 1993), 64.

God has a church. You see, we are sent by Jesus from that locked room as disciples (learners) to join him in mission, to learn by doing. Though I know we don't physically lock the doors of our church buildings on Sundays, we might often be perceived as locking the church doors behind us, in relative safety from the chaos of culture outside. The John 20 passage thus provides a striking metaphor of many disciples today, who are not living as "sent" but living behind the doors of the church building. Jesus wants us to fling open the door and live as he lived. He wants us to go outside, live a louder life, and join him in his mission.

How Are We Sent?

The logical follow-up question might be, "Then how am I sent?" Jesus clearly answers that we are sent in the same way the Father sent him. This implies we are sent in a certain fashion, sent to a specific task or place, and sent for some reason.

When you examine the Gospels and look, not for the rules and the teachings Jesus gives, but instead for the methods and environments in which he engages people, you start to notice something very interesting. First, Jesus seems to interact with people in the *normal places* of life. He walks along the road with them, he eats and drinks with them, he is in the city streets, the town squares. When we do see Jesus at the temple or synagogue, we often find him getting angry or correcting religious people. But when he is spreading the good news, living like a missionary, he is doing it in the regular rhythms of life. This is *how* the Father sent Jesus.

Second, we notice that Jesus teaches his disciples in the *everyday walks* of life. Yes, we see them together in quiet times that include prayer, sitting and teaching, and being alone, but we also see them walking the roads of the city together and engaging people with news of the kingdom. Their message of the kingdom is often communicated with examples of what the kingdom will look like, proclaiming but also demonstrating, telling but also showing. Jesus displays kingdom principles through the way he interacts with others. His basic message is that in the kingdom to come there will be no hunger, no disease, no classes of people. And so he feeds thousands, heals multitudes of diseases, and shares life with the lowest of society. The disciples are learning the ways of Jesus while they walk and live with Jesus, engaging people in common places, being sent together with him. This way of life becomes our model of sentness as well.

This rhythm of learning the ways of Jesus is in stark contrast with how we teach disciples today, in which the foremost training mechanism is the pulpit. We want people to come to an event, sit in rows, and listen to a "teaching" about a teaching. Don't hear me say I'm against the Sunday morning sermon. I still give them and enjoy listening to many I hear. However, I would suggest this is not the *best* method to learn the ways of Jesus. We have a tendency in sermons and Bible studies to emphasize and focus on the teaching of doctrines and how we should believe certain things. To discover the life out loud Jesus calls us to, we must add something to the discussions

LIFE OUT LOUD

about Jesus and our beliefs and *join* him on the road as disciples. Hugh Halter claims, "People are not looking for doctrine. They're looking for a God with skin on, a God they can know, speak with, learn from, struggle with, be honest with, get straight answers from, and connect their lives to."[16] Many of the people Jesus chose to be with were hungry, broken, poor, and marginalized in many ways. They were not looking for belief systems; they were looking for someone who could help them, be human with them. God, in Jesus, was showing the world that he would share our humanness; he would put skin on and come to walk among us.

And so, can we spend less time talking *about* walking dusty roads with Jesus, and actually get up from our pew and *join* him on those dusty roads? Really, wouldn't that be where we would find him today?

Author and theologian Richard Rohr throws cold water in the face of our church rhythms today. He writes:

> Jesus clearly taught the twelve disciples about surrender, the necessity of suffering, humility, servant leadership, and nonviolence. They resisted him every time, and so he finally had to make the journey himself and tell them, "Follow me!" But Christians have preferred to hear something Jesus never said: "Worship me."

---

16 Hugh Halter, *Flesh: Learning to Be Human Like Jesus* (Colorado Springs: David C Cook, 2014), 15.

Worship of Jesus is rather harmless and risk-free; following Jesus changes everything."[17]

Rohr is not suggesting we shouldn't worship Jesus.[18] What he is pointing out is that we've replaced everyday living and walking with Jesus in order to primarily focus on worship, something Jesus never implicitly told us to do. Not only that, we've reduced our concept of worship to the Sunday service. Worship has become an event, rather than a whole-life experience as a disciple, walking the roads with our Guide. A section in the book of Romans gives us this more complete picture of worship that includes our whole-life rhythms:

> So here's what I want you to do, God helping you: Take your everyday, ordinary life—your sleeping, eating, going-to-work, and walking-around life—and place it before God as an offering.
>
> ROMANS 12:1 (MSG)

And so, our worship lifestyle must be more than just the Sunday event. While I would certainly encourage you to be a part of a faith community that observes gathering together

---

17 Richard Rohr, "Jesus' Invitation: Follow Me," Center for Action and Contemplation, October 18, 2016. https://cac.org/jesus-invitation-follow-2016-10-18/ .

18 Clearly the disciples eventually did recognize him as more than just a rabbi or prophet, and worshiped and bowed down to him (Matthew 2:11; Matthew 14:33), and the Bible also refers to Jesus being worshiped in heaven (Hebrews 1:6).

around the sacraments, I would also say that a primary purpose of this gathering is to equip and launch you into the world as a disciple of Jesus. Missiologist Lesslie Newbigin writes, "[The church] is not meant to call men and women out of the world into a safe religious enclave but to call them out in order to send them back as agents of God's kingship."[19]

The programs on our church campus and in our church sanctuary are not the only places where your neighbors will see God at work. God shows up in the way you live, work, and play with them. Too often we are given the message to, "invite your friends to church," and it's good if they want to be with God's people and experience that gathering. However, in addition to this, *you* have been called by Jesus to demonstrate and show the gospel in your particular context of life. Today, fewer people are interested in going to church buildings to find Jesus, but that doesn't mean they're not interested in Jesus at all. Brad Brisco makes this point:

> It is we who are the called, sent missionary people of God, which will sometimes mean we must go to where people are. If we fail to go to the people, then to encounter the gospel meaningfully, they must come to us. This is the inbuilt assumption of the attractional (vendor of religious goods and services) church, and it

---

19 Lesslie Newbigin, *Foolishness to the Greeks: The Gospel and Western Culture* (Grand Rapids: Wm. B. Eerdmans Publishing, 1988), 122.

requires that the nonbeliever do the cross-cultural work to find Jesus, and not us! And make no mistake, for many people, coming to a church service involves some serious cross-cultural work. When we ask them to come to us, we are in essence asking them to be the missionaries!"[20]

Perhaps you've never stopped to think how much of a leap it is for a person who doesn't follow Jesus to come to a church building. When we realize this hurdle for others, we can then see why Jesus calls us "sent" and asks us to *go* to people in the same way he did. At the very least, we can invite them into situations with lower barriers than a church service. Perhaps your table, in your home, is the best place to show God's kingdom to others. Imagine for a moment if Jesus moved onto your street. Would Jesus invite your neighbors to a building to hear him speak, or might he invite them to his house for a meal? Our conversations all too often point to a church building rather than pointing to the road, walking with Jesus himself.

A New Pair of Shoes

Chauncey LaBrie is a pastor and activist for the kingdom in Colorado Springs, CO. In addition to his staff position in a

---

20 Brad Brisco, "Rethinking the Missionary Nature of the Church," Send Institute, May 31, 2018. https://www.sendinstitute.org/rethinking-the-missionary-nature-of-the-church/ .

church, he formed a non-profit to reach into the poor and middle-class neighborhoods in which he lives and is called to bring the gospel. Chauncey believes that when he solves physical and emotional struggles in people's lives, he is actually communicating something about the kingdom values of Jesus. When people need food, by feeding them he shows them that in the kingdom there is plenty. When a single mom needs transportation for her and her kids, by providing a van he communicates that in the kingdom she is seen and cared for.

Not long ago, Chauncey invited me to witness a kingdom statement in an under-privileged elementary school. When I arrived, I learned that, the previous Friday, Chauncey and a group of his friends and supporters had measured every shoe size of every child in that school, some 500 children. The day I was there, we had the privilege of handing out new shoes to every one of those children. Grade by grade they marched into the gymnasium as we cheered, clapped and created a party. They lined up and we handed each child a pair of brand new shoes in a bag with their name written on it. In return, we received high fives, hugs and huge smiles.

While the passing out of shoes to communicate a basic message of the kingdom was in itself a great achievement, I was struck by the simplicity, yet power, of the discipleship Chauncey was modeling. Here was one man, with a vision of communicating the kingdom in a certain way. He had invited and included twenty-five other Christians into this mission.

We had all been discipled, not by a great sermon from Chauncey, but simply by him saying, "Come join me." In passing out shoes, we were following him; we were learning a way of the gospel outside of the pulpit and a church building.

When Jesus told us we were "sent" as he was sent, we were in a sense given a new pair of shoes. It's as if he handed us shoes with our name on them. He didn't just teach about it; he told us to go and do likewise, to pass out shoes and teach others to pass out shoes. And he wasn't just passing out dress shoes for Sunday church; he was passing out sneakers and boots, shoes that would hold up for the dusty road of following him, not just attending worship services.

So what kind of shoes do you wear? Is your faith defined more by the dress shoes in your closet, or by the rugged boots designed for sentness, sturdy enough to withstand the miles of walking and following? Maybe you need a new pair of shoes.

You are a missionary! Jesus calls you "sent!" So whether in Nigeria or your neighborhood, Sudan or the soccer stadium, El Salvador or the everyday places you live, you have been sent by Jesus as a carrier of the gospel…you are a missionary.

ONE LOUDER STEP

Write down the places you already live, work, and play in, as contexts where you can live as a missionary. Start with small, intentional steps of engaging people and demonstrating the love of the kingdom. Get to know your neighbors, invite a co-worker to lunch and find out their story, take a meal to a family in need and talk about their journey. Perhaps pray with them.

3

Breakfast with Larry

Our family has a tradition of going on summer vacations to the Southern California coast. We'll find a rental home or condo somewhere south of Los Angeles and north of San Diego. Days are spent going to the beach, sightseeing, and wandering the land of the Beach Boys. On one of those family trips, my wife and I decided to go for breakfast early one morning while everyone slept in. Kitty was feeling the need for a McDonald's bacon, egg, and cheese biscuit, a rare but intense urge she sometimes has. While I'm not usually a huge fan of Ronald's place, this seemed like a worthy goal, so we set out very early in the morning in search of the glow of the Golden Arches. As we entered, I walked directly to the counter and began scanning the menu for my own stomach's desire. I turned to check with Kitty that we were ready to order, but she was no longer behind me. I looked across the dining area to see her talking with an elderly gentleman sitting at a table with his wheelchair next to him. I noticed from his worn clothing and a rough-looking napsack that Kitty's new friend was probably homeless and taking a break from the outside world. Now if you know Kitty, you know this kind of action is not unexpected. She is often the kind-hearted soul who will stop and befriend people who are sometimes overlooked. I walked over to the booth, and Kitty quickly said, "Rowland, meet my friend Larry." I introduced myself, shook his hand and asked if he would like anything to eat while I was ordering. He told us he'd love a couple of chocolate chip cookies and some more coffee. I went to the counter, presented our to-go order, along with Larry's coffee and cookies, and took it back to the table. We stood there for a moment and chatted with Larry as he sat in the booth, one leg missing, telling us a little about himself. We found out he was homeless and lived around the Mission Bay area and sometimes downtown San Diego, wherever the bus route took him. He was warm and friendly with a good sense of humor, and I was amazed by his happy outlook on life, in spite of his circumstances. We asked Larry if there was anything in particular we could do for him, and he quickly showed us the seat of his wheelchair. It comprised an old belt and some cloth, tied around the frame in such a way that he could sit on them. Basically, there was no seat. I made a couple of suggestions of how he might cheaply fix the seat, and then we left Larry the cash in our pocket and some more McDonald's and wished him well.

As Kitty and I drove back in the direction of the rental house, where our kids were still sleeping, we both felt a sense that we hadn't done enough. There we were, on a pretty sweet vacation, and while we had certainly engaged with Larry and encouraged him with some kind words, we felt we could have done more. I told Kitty to look on her phone for the nearest medical supply store. We found one less than ten miles away and drove to it as quickly as possible. When we arrived, we urgently asked the store owner for any used, nicer wheelchairs they might have in the back, anything with a seat. He rolled out a decent chair for $80, which next to Larry's looked like a Rolls Royce. We explained it was for a homeless gentleman we had just met, which led him to say they often took trade-ins on wheelchairs, then sold them or donated them to charity. I thanked him for the great price (wheelchairs can cost hundreds of dollars), and went on with a short version of our story of meeting Larry, and how we were rushing back to give it to him. As we were at the counter, as if he wanted to join our story he said, "That's really nice, you can just have it."

After thanking the shop owner, Kitty and I quickly loaded up the wheelchair in the back of our SUV and raced back to McDonald's. We were like little kids, so excited to present this to Larry and really love him well. On the way back, Kitty wrote out a card to give him with the wheelchair:

Larry, Jesus loves you. You wanted coffee and
two chocolate chip cookies, but he wanted you

to have a new wheelchair because he sees you, and he wants you to know that he loves you. Jesus really loves you and cares so much about your needs, and we love you too, Larry.

—Kitty and Rowland

We decided Kitty would go in and get him, bring him out to the car, and we'd unveil it like a birthday present or something. As I got the wheelchair out and ready, Kitty went inside. She quickly came back out with a puzzled look on her face…he was gone. We drove all around the area, behind the mall where the McDonald's was. We even stopped at a local library, and the staff told us where the homeless typically hung out. We went inside all the stores, searching for any signs, looking for over two hours. But we just couldn't find Larry.

Deflated, we drove back to our rental house with the wheelchair in the back of the SUV. We decided we'd keep it in the car on vacation and try to find someone to donate it to. Each morning, one or both of us would drive to McDonald's and see if Larry was there, but to no avail. He'd disappeared from sight, and we surrendered to the possibility we might never find him.

Sometimes It Takes a Table

Why did our encounter with Larry feel so God-ordained, like we were truly living into our sentness as his disciples? Maybe it wasn't just the "why" we loved Larry, but it was the "how" as well. We had imitated our Rabbi Jesus in his method. We were

trying to bring healing into Larry's specific physical brokenness by saying, "In the kingdom, you will not need this wheelchair, but until then, here's a better one." We also connected
with Larry around a table, albeit a McDonald's booth, but still
a table with food on it. This became a place of relationship
building, where we got to know Larry and he got to know us.

It's interesting that in the Gospels, we're given three statements about Jesus' coming. He came:

1. to seek and save the lost [21]
2. to serve and not be served, and give his life as a ransom
   for many[22]
3. eating and drinking.[23]

We know Jesus' purpose: to seek and save the lost. We
know his posture: servanthood. But we often forget his entry
point: the table. The first two seem to fit the nature and image
of the Son of God, the God we hear about in church so often.
They are very theological and fit our religious language well.
The third one, however, seems out of place for some reason.
The table was a tool for announcing his kingdom.[24] Luke's
Gospel records five times that Jesus eats with others, and in the
Scriptures we see many other examples where Jesus chooses a
meal as a connection point.

---

21 Luke 19:10.
22 Matthew 20:28.
23 Luke 7:34.
24 Thomas Thompson, "Sometimes It Takes a Table: Everyone Is Invited," Pulpit
Rock Church, September 3, 2017. http://pulpitrock.com/sometimes-it-takes-a-ta-
ble-everyone-is-invited/ .

The table can seem like a strange place for the Son of God to do his kingdom business. Tim Chester makes the point that the Jews of the day would have said the Messiah will come in glory and in power, to defeat God's enemies. They never would have expected him to come eating and drinking, with sinners and tax collectors.[25] A table doesn't seem like a holy place, in comparison to a church sanctuary. You don't often hear the method of eating and drinking spoken of in the pulpit, unless it involves a church social. It just doesn't seem very strategic, and so in our teachings it's rarely associated with Jesus.

However, Kitty and I have learned how important tables can be. They aren't just pieces of furniture, but they are places of community and love. Whether it's a group of young adults breaking bread and pasta for an evening meal in America, or an extended family eating lamb and couscous in Northern Africa, the table is a place that defines family. A table with food is disarming, it's transparent, it's life-sharing, and everyone around it is not only eye-level but they are life-level in posture and identity. The table is a place where people sit facing each other, *imago Dei* to *imago Dei*. Perhaps this is why Jesus often used a table in the rhythms of his life and ministry. And so, maybe the table is less of a *metaphor* for ministry and more of an actual *method* for ministry. Jesus knew something about tables we often miss. A table is a way to live as the sent people of God. They are places of relationship, culture, and belonging.

---

25 Tim Chester, *A Meal with Jesus: Discovering Grace, Community & Mission around the Table* (Wheaton: Crossway, 2011), 12.

Leonard Sweet writes, "At the table, where food and stories are passed from one person to another, and one generation to another, is where each of us learns who we are, what we can be, to whom we belong, and to what we are called."[26] This deeper meaning of the table is something that was true in Jesus' day and is still true in ours. Real belonging, real membership is found around a table, and so Jesus came eating and drinking.

What infuriated Jesus' religious contemporaries is *with whom* he ate. They would have expected the Messiah to sit on a throne, surrounded by the religious leaders of piety, yet we find Jesus sitting with sinners, tax collectors, prostitutes, and others considered to be on the fringes of society. This was Jesus' way of showing people they were included in the kingdom of God, not because of any behavior or status, but because he loved them in spite of their behavior and brokenness. Their dignity was found in him; their invitation was because he invited them. Thomas Thompson says, "You are with whom you break bread."[27] When we share a table with other *imago Dei*, then we live out the reality that we too need Jesus' invitation to commune with him. Regardless of social structures, belief systems, behaviors, or fallenness, we *all* need a seat at the table.

Jesus shared his presence at the table, sitting with people

---

26 Leonard Sweet, *From Tablet to Table: Where Community Is Found and Identity Is Formed* (Colorado Springs: Navpress, 2014), 8.

27 Thomas Thompson, Pulpit Rock Church, 2017, http://pulpitrock.com/sometimes-it-takes-a-table-everyone-is-invited/ .

to bring a message of life and restoration. As he broke bread with the broken, he spoke of life and a new kingdom. As he drank wine with those who were thirsty, he offered a cup that quenched the dryness of life. Jesus used a table, sitting eye to eye with those who needed him most. Sharing food was to share life, and sharing the road to life was the reason Jesus came. Next time you think you should invite your neighbor to church, perhaps instead consider asking them to your own table, backyard BBQ, or kitchen as a place you "do church." Yes, invitations may include a Sunday gathering with a larger community worship service, but feel the freedom to do ministry the way Jesus did, with food and a table. Eating food together and opening up our table means we are sharing our life with others and them with us. It's a simple way to learn to love our neighbor in the context of something we do multiple times a day. Meals need not be fancy—they just need to be shared.

Tables are all around us—in our home, in coffee shops, in restaurants, in parks, in all the places where we live, work, and play. What if we deliberately lived our lives around food and around the table? When we intentionally seek out tables, we will find the gift of people like Larry. We'll find new relationships to live into. We'll start seeing the places where we can love our neighbor. We'll find simple ways to represent Jesus to others. Our own lives will be blessed as we join God in announcing his kingdom in practical ways. He might even invite us to heal someone's life and pain in a major way…or at least get them a wheelchair.

King for a Day

I remember the first time I was invited to go with my dad to have lunch with Witt Stephens. Mr. Stephens was legendary. He and his brother Jack built an investment brokerage business in Little Rock, Arkansas from the ground up, and it was well respected by many. Living in the shadows of large New York companies, Stephens Inc. held on to its Southern roots and heritage, and was, for a time, the largest brokerage firm "off" Wall Street. Mr. Witt, as he was affectionately known by his friends, was a man you wanted to be around. You wanted to hang on his every word and catch any pieces of wisdom that might be uttered without warning. My dad had worked for Stephens Inc. for a time, before launching his own private investment advisory firm. Mr. Witt was like a mentor to him, and had taken him under his wing in many ways.

I remember when Dad told me to wear my best suit the next day because we were having lunch at Stephens Inc. This was momentous for me. I can recall going up in the private elevator with Dad all the way to the top floor, into the restricted area of the Stephens brothers' offices. They had their own dining room, which also served as a boardroom. It was just as I imagined during my sleepless night before: dark wood everywhere, expensive furniture, books lining the walls, and chairs that smelled of leather and creaked when you sat in them. Mr. Witt walked in, and we both jumped to our feet and shook hands with him as he graciously welcomed us. I used a firm handshake, just as my dad had reminded me on the elevator ride up. We sat together at the big, dark, oak table. As if on cue, two butlers came in, wearing white coats, and took our drink orders. The fare was the best of Arkansas beef and included choosing dessert from a mobile butler-powered cart. Conversations weaved in and out of personal family history, Arkansas wild-tales, duck hunting stories, and predictions on the direction of interest rates and the markets. Those two hours were incredible—the invitation to sit at this particular table brought me into a whole new world. I was part of a new community that now included the legendary Mr. Witt. I also saw my dad in a whole new light as I watched him banter back and forth about the stock and bond markets with one of the best financial minds around. In a sense, my father had invited me to eat at the king's table.

A Seat at the Table

There's a person in the Bible I love to regularly return to and read about. He has an odd name and a very interesting story, not too removed from my experience with Mr. Witt. He too had a king's table story. His name was Mephibosheth.

To learn about Mephibosheth, you have to go back into the Old Testament and read a couple of passages. One of these introductions to him is just a quick parenthetical mention. We learn in 2 Samuel 4:4 that King Saul's son, Jonathan, had a son named Mephibosheth:

(Jonathan son of Saul had a son who was lame in both feet. He was five years old when the news about Saul and Jonathan came from Jezreel. His nurse picked him up and fled, but as she hurried to leave, he fell and became disabled. His name was Mephibosheth.)

2 SAMUEL 4:4

Right after you read that verse, there's no immediate mention of Mephibosheth. It seems out of place and kind of strange, until you get to 2 Samuel 9. To understand what's going on next, you have to know the backstory of David, and his history with King Saul and Jonathan.

David was chosen by God to eventually be the king of Israel. Saul, who was king when David was prophetically chosen, didn't like the idea of someone else taking his throne. This led to a rivalry, with Saul wanting to kill David. However, David respected Saul as the king God had in power at that moment. Saul would chase David with his army and try to kill him. Even though David knew he had been chosen to be king, and even with opportunity to kill Saul, David did not take Saul's death into his own hands, allowing God to choose the timing of what had been prophesied over him as a child. You must also be introduced to Saul's son, Jonathan, who was a great friend of David's. They were like brothers, and even though Jonathan's father wanted to see David killed, Jonathan did not, and often stood up for him, in a secret brother-like relationship between them.

Saul and Jonathan both met their death at the battle of Mount Gilboa, allowing David to begin his rise in taking the throne over Israel and Judah.[28] When we reach 2 Samuel 9, we see David as king, inquiring if there are any family members left from the house of Saul. Ziba, a past servant of Saul, is brought before David and is asked, "Is there no one still alive from the house of Saul to whom I can show God's kindness?" (2 Samuel 9:3). Ziba tells him there is a son of Jonathan left, but he is lame in both feet. Now our parenthetical verse from 2 Samuel 4 makes sense! Mephibosheth had been dropped by his nurse as a child, which resulted in him being lame for the rest of his life—he couldn't walk. After all these years, Mephibosheth, forgotten about by time, is found by David inquiring who in Saul's family might still be alive. Mephibosheth is brought before David:

> David said, "Mephibosheth!"
> "At your service," he replied.
> "Don't be afraid," David said to him, "for I will surely show you kindness for the sake of your father Jonathan. I will restore to you all the land that belonged to your grandfather Saul, and you will always eat at my table."
> Mephibosheth bowed down and said, "What is your servant, that you should notice a dead dog like me?"
> 2 SAMUEL 9:6–8

---

28 See 2 Samuel 1–2.

Mephibosheth's description of himself as a "dead dog" gives us a clue, not only of how he was viewed in society, but also how he was likely viewed in the order of Saul's family line. Being lame in both feet would not have gone unnoticed. His lameness would have brought shame on his family, and he would have been regarded as less than fully capable; he had no chance of taking the throne in succession. While his bloodline ensured he was taken care of at someone's home, he did not live in the king's house.[29] In calling himself a "dead dog," Mephibosheth clearly feels the cultural shame of his infirmity.

David's response is perhaps one of the most heartwarming stories in Scripture. With Mephibosheth's head hung low, and his identity as a dog of society, David responds:

> Then the king summoned Ziba, Saul's steward, and said to him, "I have given your master's grandson everything that belonged to Saul and his family. You and your sons and your servants are to farm the land for him and bring in the crops, so that your master's grandson may be provided for. And Mephibosheth, grandson of your master, will always eat at my table."
>
> 2 SAMUEL 9:9–10

We have dogs in our house, sometimes too many. If my daughter leaves her dog for a few days, and my son's dog is

---

29 "David had him brought from Lo Debar, from the house of Makir son of Ammiel" (2 Samuel 9:5).

running around with ours, we can have four of them, sitting at the foot of the table, just waiting on scraps to be dropped. This would be the life of the lame, waiting on the scraps of society to stay alive.

At the word of the king, Mephibosheth is lifted from the floor under the table where the scraps fall. He is given all his grandfather's assets, as well as his servants. He is also given something prized above all those things: a seat at the king's table. This lame, dead dog, who you could say lived off the scraps of the king's table, is given a seat at the table instead of the floor. The story finishes with a new identity for Mephibosheth:

> And Mephibosheth lived in Jerusalem, because
> he always ate at the king's table; he was lame in
> both feet.
>
> 2 SAMUEL 9:13

Again, the writer of 2 Samuel, for some reason, makes note that a person who was lame was invited to always eat at the king's table, as if to emphasize the unlikeliness of this situation.

Everybody's Lame

When we encounter people who are struggling in life, whether physically, emotionally, or spiritually, we have the opportunity to join God in radically changing their identity, the way ours has been changed by Jesus. More often than not, they are aware of the shortfalls in their life. They know their struggles, they know their identity, and have often mistaken their true identity for one of shame. Often, they may see themselves internally like a dead dog of society, even though they are acting like life is fine on the outside. Sometimes, to see themselves differently, as worthy of a king's table, might just take an invitation from you. For them to be lifted up and to sit at a table with you moves God's love from theoretical to actual. A simple chair can powerfully communicate, "You are loved, and worthy of more than scraps."

As the "sent" people of King Jesus, we get to play the part of Ziba from Mephibosheth's story, seeking those who metaphorically feel lame and inviting them into the presence of the King. As the representatives of Jesus, sent as the Father sent him, we get to invite and host them at the King's table, which is also our table. Of course, we all have our own lameness to contend with. We may have our own stories of being invited to the King's table, in spite of our crippled condition. Because of our personal stories of invitation, we have the joy of inviting others, showing them there is a seat with their name on it.

Mephibosheth Found!

On the last day of our vacation, Kitty and I decided to make one last run to McDonald's very early in the morning. We parked the truck and walked inside to grab breakfast. As we opened the door and looked to the left, there was Larry. We couldn't believe it! We were so excited and ran over to him like long-lost relatives. To this day I'm still not sure if he remembered who we were at that moment. We looked like a couple of crazies: two white, middle-class parents running over to an obviously homeless guy at a table, shouting his name and waving our arms. We resisted the urge to grab and hug him, though we desperately wanted to. He then quickly remembered us and displayed a big smile on his life-worn face.

We asked Larry what he wanted for breakfast, our habit with him now, and we all sat down to McDonald's like it was a grade-A Arkansas beef dinner and we were old friends. I began to ask Larry more about his life, and he started sharing stories—of working in Chicago, and how his leg was lost in a train accident. We found out about his past family and his life on the streets. After a while, it occurred to us that we had forgotten the best part! I ran out to the car to get the wheelchair, leaving Kitty inside with Larry—we weren't going to let him out of our sight again! I opened the doors and brought back in an almost new wheelchair for him. He looked at this shiny piece of equipment like it was a sports car. Compared to the chair he had been living in, it looked brand new. He was incredibly grateful, expressed by the huge smile on his face, and Kitty got her long-awaited hug. She also got her picture taken with Larry standing next to the wheelchair, balancing on his one leg, both of them arm in arm. We hung that picture on our wall, and it's there to this day in a frame with the words "Love Much" printed on it. Taped to the back of it is a duplicate card with the words Kitty wrote to Larry. We often think of him like he's part of our family in some way. No doubt he is part of our family's story. Though he doesn't eat with us anymore, we like to think he always has a seat at our table with his name on it, should we ever meet again. We often talk about vacationing in San Diego, just so we can go to McDonald's and, just maybe, sit at the King's table together one more time.

We have two walls in our house on which we hang crosses we've collected from around the world. A few were made by our kids as well. They are colorful, artsy, and all different sizes and materials, but they are the same shape: a cross. We hung Larry's picture on that wall with those crosses because it reminds us that Jesus loves us much, and so we love others with the same intent. Larry has always been a pinnacle lesson for us in our faith. Though we blessed Larry with a wheelchair, he blessed us by allowing us to eat with him, and share some of our life and time with him. People may come in all colors and sizes, and all walks of life, or may be unable to walk life well because of their lameness, but they all have the same identity ...*imago Dei*. Kitty and I learned something about humanity that week, and about God. It didn't take a Bible study, or a sermon, or a memory verse; all it took was a table, and breakfast with Larry.

After Kitty and I had our brief Mephibosheth moments with Larry, his physical lameness continued. Though we were able to get him a better seat at the table in the form of a new wheelchair, he still struggled with physical lameness, homelessness, and I can imagine some loneliness. Still, our opportunity when we noticed him, was to offer him a seat at the table. The table was in McDonald's, which is far from food fit for a king, but it served the purpose of helping Larry realize he has a seat at the table of humanity, at the table of Jesus, because two of Jesus' people invited him to sit there. Perhaps it's a stretch for you to consider it this way, but Kitty and I like to think that the message to Larry was simply, "Jesus sees you, because two of his disciples see you." In his "dead-dogness," Larry was noticed by Jesus because we, those sent by Jesus, noticed him. My hope is that Larry felt like I did that day in Mr. Witt's office. I hope instead of a laminated booth in McDonald's, it felt like a big, dark, oak table with butlers. It's moments like these that shape our lives and can shape the lives of others. I still remember that day with Mr. Witt. I can smell the cigar smoke after lunch; I can hear the echoes of my dad and him, bouncing off the old oak bookcases. When you take the time to use a table and love people, you invite them into moments they will remember. They will recall the smells, the sounds, the community. It will smell like love; it will sound like someone saying, "You're not lame," "You're not damaged goods," "You're worthy of a spot at the table."

Jesus regularly used the table to engage people. Food and fellowship brought them together. You may not be able to change someone's circumstances or issues in life, but my hope and prayer is that, like Ziba, you see yourself as a partner with the King, inviting someone to their real identity. I hope you not only start noticing the Mephibosheths of society, those who have been thrown away to the margins because of their lameness, but I hope you also start offering them a seat at your table. Grab a calendar and pick a date to invite your neighbors to dinner; ask that co-worker or approach that broken person you know who needs to see a chair with their name on it. Your life out loud may not be with the homeless at a McDonald's. It may be a walk across the street, asking someone to your own kitchen table or backyard grill. You will find that everybody is lame in one way or another. We all have a story that could label us as "dead dogs." We all need a seat at the King's table.

ONE LOUDER STEP

Pick two or three houses or apartments surrounding you and invite the occupants, one at a time, to a meal or dessert at your house. Listen to their story. (By the way, put away your Bible and verses for the night.)

4

Salt

I love watching TV cooking shows featuring top professional chefs battling it out for the title of "Best chef." The irony is I don't really like eating fine cuisine. I'm not drawn to eating goose liver, weird animal parts, raw beef or sauces I can't pronounce. But I love watching these food artists at work! I appreciate the skill and care with which they season and put flavors together. The judges are so attuned to the slightest amount of seasoning that they know when to suggest adding "a little more garlic," or "a drizzle of lemon," or "a dash of pepper." Sometimes they will critique too much of a good thing, like too much salt.

A few years back we built a sunroom on our deck, which had become pretty worn out with age. We needed to do something before it fell down. Instead of just rebuilding it as it was, we planned a half sunroom and a partial outdoor deck, where we could invite neighbors over to eat. In the budget for our project I made sure to include a smoker/grill. We love to open our home to others, and in our minds, a grill is one of our best tools for community building. There was a particular grill I wanted, so I went to several retail outlets to find the best price and size for us. After purchasing the one I wanted and registering the warranty online, I began receiving some great emails with a whole variety of recipes—things I'd never even considered cooking on a grill. There were recipes for skillet-grilled vegetables, soup and chili, even Texas toast. On many recipes, they suggested using some of their own-branded spice mixes. They had a spice for chicken, one for beef, one for ribs, among others. After scrolling through a slew of recipes online, I decided this grill was going to be the best purchase I'd ever made! I was pretty excited and my adrenaline was rushing, so in typical fashion, I didn't read the directions or the details of a recipe, but instead just made a plan to fire it up and get grillin'.

I went to the grocery to get some brisket, then bought the spice mix that matched up with the meat. I felt like a professional BBQer getting ready for a competition. When I returned home, I fired up the smoker, got the meat out and grabbed the bottle of spice mix. It said "rub" in the name, so I just coated the meat with it and rubbed it in every nook and cranny. It smelled very strong and my hands were turning strange colors, but I just kept sprinkling and kept rubbing. After it seemed like the meat had enough spice rub, and it started looking like the color of my hands, I took it out to the smoker and put it on the rack. As it was cooking, I decided it needed the rub a couple more times, so I brushed it on liberally. What harm could it do?

After it had slow-cooked for several hours, I took the brisket off and it looked fantastic! I was so proud and felt like a top chef. I couldn't wait to try it, so I cut the end off and popped it in my mouth. To say that it was over-seasoned would be an understatement. With my eyes watering, I choked down that little piece of meat. Now, I'm a big fan of the crusty part that forms on the outside of smoked and grilled meat. I had been successful in creating a great-looking dark crust on the outside of the brisket, but it was the crust that had been over-seasoned. The meat on the inside was ok, so I cut the crust off, and we ate our first smoked brisket off the new grill.

Since having this smoker, I've learned how to season different meats with various rubs and flavors. I've learned how much to use, and more importantly, how much *not* to use. Seasoning is somewhat of an art: too much will overwhelm the end result; too little and it doesn't bring out the flavor.

The Bible talks about salt and seasoning. In fact, salt is referred to about fifty-four times in Scripture. It had significant practical uses in biblical times, but the metaphorical connections to our faith are amazing and speak loudly into our missional discussion.

In one of these salt passages, Jesus gives a cautionary warning:

"You are the salt of the earth. But if the salt loses its saltiness, how can it be made salty again? It is no longer good for anything, except to be thrown out and trampled underfoot."

MATTHEW 5:13

I'll be honest, for years the "salt passages" were pretty confusing to me. I had read and heard a myriad of different interpretations about salt, what it was, what it meant, and the implications for how we live a Christian life. I have always known that salt tastes good and adds flavor to things. I also learned that salt was a preservative, and was used on meat and other foods in a time before refrigeration. But I never understood how I should view salt as a metaphor in the same way the writers of Scripture did.

I remember right after becoming a Christian, sitting in that first church I was baptized in, listening to the pastor warn me about losing my saltiness. According to him, and at first glance of the passage above, I needed to be careful not to look like the world, or stray too far from the truth. After all, if I lost my saltiness, well…who wants to be trampled underfoot! We were encouraged to be salt by being a visible and verbal reminder of where the world stopped and God started. Salt, holiness, preserved our way of life as Christians, and so to be too close to the world or culture was to lose your saltiness. Many theologians over time have focused on salt as a metaphor for preserving the kingdom and the values of the kingdom. Salt is considered to be exhibited by our beliefs and doctrines. If we follow this thinking, then we can easily find ourselves, as salty people, critiquing where the culture has gone astray and commenting on which laws and social discourse are ungodly. As we verbally correct society and culture about the way they are living, we preserve the culture we want as Christians, and this is what we have commonly considered to be "living as salt."

This never felt very much like "seasoning" to me though. If you're familiar with those blue salt containers you purchase at the grocery, then you're probably aware that some come with holes on one side and a pour spout on the other. As Christians, and as the church, we often operate more like a pour spout, dumping salt on any issues that feel countercultural to our values. We pour as much salt as we can in 280 characters on Twitter; we see preachers on television being interviewed about culture, taking out their verbal salt and dumping as much as they can in a ten-minute conversation. Creating mountains of salt to cover up cultural disagreements has given the church a bad name. We are now often excluded from the conversation because when someone else opens their mouth to explain their opinion, more often than not, we pull out the pour spout and fill their mouth with sodium, causing them to just spit us, and our "holiness," out.

When you reread Matthew 5:13 in the context of the whole discourse in Matthew, you pick up something interesting.

"You are the salt of the earth. But if the salt loses its saltiness, how can it be made salty again?

It is no longer good for anything, except to be thrown out and trampled underfoot. You are the light of the world. A town built on a hill cannot be hidden. Neither do people light a lamp and put it under a bowl. Instead they put it on its stand, and it gives light to everyone in the house. In the same way, let your light shine before others, that they may see your good deeds and glorify your Father in heaven."

MATTHEW 5:13–16

Jesus is talking here about being "salt" and being "light" all in one instruction and movement. When you see this as one whole instruction, then the final phrase can relate to both being salt and light: "that they may see your good deeds and glorify your Father in heaven." In the same teaching, Jesus says that we let our light shine by our good deeds, not by shining a floodlight on all that culture is doing wrong, but by living as light into darkness with our good actions. In the same way, we are salt, not by drowning the sins of culture in a judgmental mountain of white sodium, but by living and showing the kingdom in places that are counter-kingdom. What Jesus seems to be saying is that we are light and salt by the way in which we represent the kingdom through our actions, not primarily by preserving the rules of it. We draw people into the kingdom by winsomely seasoning their life with kingdom deeds. Being salt is about bringing good taste to things in the world that may have lost the flavor of God's kingdom. Being salt in the kingdom is about being the cook, knowing what to season, when, and how much.

Reggie McNeal writes of this passage:

> It is impossible for missional Jesus followers to read these verses without a quickened heartbeat. These powerful metaphors show us what it means to be the people of God in the world. Salt penetrates, permeates, and preserves. All of these functions require its presence. It is not a neutral presence. Salt is an active ingredient that changes the flavor of things. The light metaphor illustrates the obvious truth that light shines in darkness. But it also adds the additional promise that when the people of God act like the people of God, we actually help people see God."[30]

When we act like the people of God, people can see God, and experience his kingdom. Acting as the people of God is to season with salt and grant a taste of God's kingdom where the world needs to taste good.

In his letter to the church in Colossae, in what is now western Turkey, Paul writes:

> Walk in wisdom toward outsiders, making the best use of the time. Let your speech always be

---

30 Reggie McNeal, *Missional Renaissance: Changing the Scorecard* (San Francisco: Josey-Bass, 2009), 33.

gracious, seasoned with salt, so that you may
know how you ought to answer each person.

COLOSSIANS 4:5–6 (ESV)

Paul seems to understand Jesus' intent on being salt (and
light). He is instructing this faith community to be wise in
how they season their speech with outsiders (those who don't
follow Jesus yet). He adds the example that seasoning speech
with salt accompanies gracious speech.

Soon after becoming a Christian, I understood the last
part of the verse, "…so that you may know how you ought to
answer each person." I understood that knowing the right biblical answer was how I would protect myself from the world.
I rarely, if ever, thought about gracious speech being the de-
livery method. What I sometimes heard from the pulpit was
that we needed to separate ourselves from the world. We were
taught how to differentiate between the salty and non-salty
parts of life; the secular and the sacred, the holy and unholy.
When we hold this kind of mindset, we can easily become
critical and judgmental of others, pouring out "holiness" on
cultural issues of disagreement.

If we approach seasoning our conversations in this way,
it can often feel to others like too much rub on the meat. But
I've come to realize we are called to so much more than merely
guarding the faith. We don't need to live defensively, nor do we
need to be overly offensive towards the places or people we disagree with. We can simply live as good cooks, trying to season

with salt in the places we inhabit. As I said, cooking is an art. It can be hard to discern how much and when to season. When it comes to salt, the idiom breaks down: you *can* have too much of a good thing.

Though we don't want to walk around with big blue canisters of salt, we also don't want to be absent of saltshakers, blending into culture with no discernible identity. Speaking into this issue, Mike Frost coined the phrase, "living 'questionable' lives." As followers of Jesus, we are meant to live a life that is a "godly, intriguing, socially adventurous, joyous presence in the lives of others."[31] Such a life evokes curiosity and causes those around us to question why we do the things we do and why we live the way we live. So often, our words can carry the sting of venom, and our lives look like every other neighbor on the block. Our lives are far from intriguing and inviting; they are status quo. What if our habits were like a saltshaker in the hands of a master chef, seeking to give a taste of the kingdom in the ways we lived amongst our neighbors? What if, at our hands, the marginalized were included, the abused were protected, the poor were fed, the neighbor was loved and cared for? Might people be intrigued with our faith? Might they question why we live that way, care so much, and why we love so much? Gracious words might also be equated to gracious actions, and gracious living might then be equated to Jesus being present in our life. What might need to change in your own life in order to live a questionable life? A

---

31 Michael Frost, *Surprise the World: The Five Habits of Highly Missional People* (Colorado Springs: Navpress, 2016), 13.

life where others see you and your actions as "tasting good" in the midst of a world that often tastes over-seasoned?

I Have a Verse

I look back on my first years of being a Christian and shake my head at the ways I tried to announce the kingdom to others. I remember thinking I needed to memorize the cookbook (the Bible) so that I could defend God at a moment's notice. The first Bible I bought was huge. It had all the normal verses in it, and it was also filled with maps, commentaries, history, and so on. It was also red, really red. I remember carrying this monstrosity with pride…I also remember all the friendships I lost by using it as a weapon upon their way of life. Truth, salt, could be riddled out like machine gun fire whenever God or Christian values were challenged.

Perhaps one of the worst things we've taught people is how to have a verse for everything, to be able to say, "I have a verse for that." When we use Scripture in this way, we risk taking a single verse out of context from the writing, conversation, or poetry it was presented in. Having verses "ready" for cultural issues can also lead to using the Scriptures negatively instead of communicating the proactive story of God redeeming the world, redeeming others, and redeeming us. What if, instead of arming ourselves with pithy verses, we're ready to tell whole stories, whole parables, summaries of God and his people, so that we can encourage others or tell someone how God sees them as an image of him. Perhaps we'd start living out the kingdom of God in a different way. Instead of justifying something with a verse, or discrediting something else with another verse, we might draw others into the bigger story of God, which invites us all to wrestle with life toward wholeness and redemption.

I remember the day I walked into our coffee shop and saw a lady playing cards at our large community table. I could have sworn from a distance she was playing Solitaire, so I walked over to check on her and thank her for being in our space. When I approached her, I noticed she was deeply focused on Tarot cards. At first, this set me back on my mental heels, but then I found the courage to ask her what she was doing. As she explained the Tarot card system to me, and how she was seeking some answers to an issue in her life, I found myself strangely connected to her, not by beliefs, but by our common story of using spiritual matters to seek answers in life. After we'd chatted for about five minutes, she asked me an unexpected question: "How do you find answers to things?" Trying not to stumble over my own theology, I told her that I followed "a guy named Jesus and his teachings." I went on to explain that he taught about loving others, and about the way to life and light. She countered, and explained that she grew up in church, but it was too judgmental for her. We talked for about twenty minutes about our spiritual ideas. While she didn't say a prayer to follow Jesus right at that moment, she expressed she had never met a pastor like me before. I took it as a compliment, and as evidence I'd perhaps reformed from my previous abusive red-Bible days. I had several verses at my disposal on why she shouldn't be reading Tarot cards. I could have pulled out my spiritual saltshaker and heaped saltiness all over her cards. Instead, by leading with love for another person seeking answers, I caused her to look at me with intrigue, a Christian she wasn't used to. A monologue against Tarot cards would have shut the conversation down before it even started. I needed to simply sit with her at the table, not allowing my uneasiness about her Tarot cards to kill the discussion. Maybe this particular encounter with a Christian left her curious. I hope so.

When we "arm" Christ-followers with verbal truth but don't teach them how to be wise and gracious in speech (and action), we inadvertently create judgmental Christianity, not based on grace, but based on people not living up to the rules and verses we have stored away. The fact of the matter is, we ourselves struggle to live up to those verses. Rules-based, verse-based religion is precisely the type of religion that Jesus came to redefine. It's not that Scripture is unimportant, or that the Bible is not foundational to our walk with the Lord, but it was never meant to be a code book or a rule book. The Scriptures give us seasonings of how God lives with his people and with the world. We see the struggles of people trying to understand who God is, and how he wants to make them his, and how he is their God. We read the history, the poetry, the songs, the prophecies, the narrative of a people being seasoned with the story of the kingdom. God's inspired Scriptures pull on our heartstrings to join in the bigger story of being his people and sharing the mission to love others into the kingdom.

The Salt Between Us

While salt was a preserving agent in biblical times, it was also significant as a sign of covenant making. Salt was the symbol of a binding agreement. The word *salary*, for example, comes from the word for "salt-money," referring to the price a soldier was paid in order to purchase an allowance of salt. Today, we receive a salary for the work we do, a covenant of salt. Maybe you've heard at times that someone who is worth their salary is said to be "worth their salt."

Throughout the Old Testament of Scripture, we see instructions for adding salt to offerings for God as a symbol of covenant. In the book of Leviticus we find an example of this covenant of salt:

> Season all your grain offerings with salt. Do not leave the salt of the covenant of your God out of your grain offerings; add salt to all your offerings.
>
> LEVITICUS 2:13

There would obviously be no need to preserve grain with salt, but it was used in offerings to symbolize the enduring, covenantal nature of the relationship with God. To add salt to your offering was to say to God that your devotion and worship were preserved and long-lasting.

There is an Arabic phrase that says, "There is salt between us" or "He has eaten of my salt."[32] It shows the power of salt in symbolizing strong relationships between two parties that have formed a covenant, even if they were formerly enemies. Salt was the way two people exchanged a vow of friendship. It was more than a taste enhancer: it was an important symbol of friendship and a preserved covenant. This cultural symbol gives some context to a salt Scripture in the Gospel of Mark, where he writes:

> Salt is good, but if it loses its saltiness, how can you make it salty again? Have salt among yourselves, and be at peace with each other.

> MARK 9:50

Being at peace with our neighbor shows we have salt within us; it shows a preserved quality of the kingdom. Having salt within, and being at peace, gives us the mental picture of what it looks like to live out that most important quality of a Jesus person: to love God and also love your neighbor.[33] In other words, a Jesus person is also a salt person. Salt shows a covenant of peace and an offering that is everlasting and preserved. When you read this in the context of the passage we looked at earlier in Matthew 5, we can see that being a

---

32 Emil G. Hirsch, Immanuel Benzinger, Cyrus Adler, M. Seligsohn, *Salt*, Jewish Encyclopedia Online, http://www.jewishencyclopedia.com/articles/13043-salt .

33 Mark 12:30–31.

person of salt is to be wise and aware in seasoning our relationships, especially with those who don't follow Jesus. This wisdom involves gracious speech and actions, as well as peace with one another. To lose one's saltiness is to lose this peaceful, gracious attitude of seasoning the world with the good tastes of the kingdom of God. If we lose this way of living as a Christ-follower, we might as well be trampled underfoot…our "salt" is no longer good for anything. I don't know about you, but this visual is very different to the one I was taught early in my Christian journey.

The Talmud is a written collection of teachings from Jewish rabbis, compiled over centuries, as they interpreted and taught Israel about the laws of Moses, the prophets, and other writings from what we now know as the Old Testament. In the Talmud it says, "The world can get along without pepper, but it cannot get along without salt."[34] Salt is indispensable in the life of a God-follower. Salt is a symbol of the preserved covenant we have with God. It is also the symbol of a people of peace, people who bring a taste of God's kingdom into a world that sometimes tastes wrong.

We can all learn to be good kingdom cooks! Organizations like Forge America have given me tools to consider salty living in a different light, and to be more effective at seasoning with the kingdom.[35] Over time, my red Bible has disappeared. I still carry verses by memory and have ways that I interpret

34 Yerushalmi Hora'yot 3:5.

35 https://www.forgeamerica.com .

and teach what I consider to be the truth of Scripture. But I've learned to lead with a saltshaker, not a pour spout. When we live this way, we actually find a new freedom and meaning in our faith. We start living the way Jesus did, seasoning the world with the kingdom of God.

The Sous-Chef

I love my wife, but we don't do particularly well cooking together in the kitchen. One of us has to be in charge, primarily because we each have a different way we like to do things. I might want to steam something, whereas she might want to boil it. When I'd like to grill, she would like to bake, and so on. The solution to this problem is the concept of the sous-chef. I learned about the sous-chef on those cooking shows I enjoy, and I think it saved our marriage!

The sous-chef is the second-in-command to the head chef. A good sous-chef is indispensable to the chef. They learn to think like the chef, do things like her or him, and can cook dishes and recipes in the same way the chef would prepare them. When you eat something you think the chef prepared, she might have just been overseeing the sous-chef prepare it. When Kitty and I have people over, one of us always takes the lead in cooking or grilling out. The other naturally steps into the role of sous-chef and assists.

The kingdom is a lot like this as well. God as Chef has offered us a role as sous-chef. Other people can taste the meal God has designed for them—a meal that is prepared by our hands. He invites us to season, to create, to inspire, to bring beauty and goodness into the world. He sends us out to cook just like he would: to bring peace, healing, and love, just as he would…and still does.

It took me years to learn to season correctly, in the kitchen and in my life. And I'm still learning. Every once in a while a little smoke still appears from the oven, my light is occasionally a little glaring, and my speech a little over-seasoned, but at least I'm more aware of it and can adjust my recipe. Now, I feel better equipped to walk as a Christ-follower in a world that often doesn't follow him. I don't feel like I always have to battle the world to save God. God is on his mission and I just want to join him in redeeming his world. You don't need to save God from culture—he knows what's happening. I encourage you to resist the temptation to over-season the world with truth, and instead insert gracious speech whenever you feel the urge to insert a verse. Learn to be a sous-chef instead of the head chef, following God's lead, letting him work first, and then simply join him. When you encounter someone searching for spiritual meaning, like my Tarot card friend, join the conversation about spiritual matters, sharing your perspective of Jesus and his love for everyone. Take a chance and ask a not-yet-Christ-follower, "Can I pray for that during my prayer time?" in response to their struggles in life. Bring glimpses of the kingdom when a door opens, when you can add a pinch of salt. Leave the pour spout closed.

When we let go of the need to over-season truth into a

broken world, we actually find that the world may be willing to sit at our table and taste the kingdom. When we prepare the meal carefully, then we will find that all those people made in God's image are actually searching for a better tasting world, just like you and me. But old habits are sometimes hard to break—too much knowledge is sometimes hard to keep inside. I still over-salt my food. What's true of cooking can also be true of the kingdom and of life: less can often be more.

ONE LOUDER STEP

Be attuned to neighbors or co-workers, and practice sharing a taste of the kingdom of God in small ways, leading with gracious words, shining light into dark places, and living as an example of the kingdom. Engage them in conversation and find out something about their life.

5

The Smell of the Gospel

I have a friend named Eric, whom I truly admire. He leads a church community in a quirky neighborhood in the corner of my city, Colorado Springs. The Sanctuary Church is kind of a strange church, in the best way. They are constantly asking loud questions about their presence in the neighborhood and how they can best bring glimpses of the kingdom of God to their friends and neighbors. Early on I developed a deep respect for The Sanctuary, stemming from all the weird stories I had heard about them living into their community in tangible ways. As I heard more and more unusual stories about them, I became inquisitive and wanted to find out what was happening in their building and in their neighborhood. Eric and I finally met at a pastors' gathering, and so I took the opportunity to set up lunch and go see what I had been hearing so much about.

When I arrived at The Sanctuary, I immediately noticed it was nestled right in between Colorado Avenue, the main drag through Old Colorado City, and a school. It is an old stone church building with a pretty nice vibe to it, and a strong, visible presence to the residents of the area. As Eric took me on a tour of their building, we began walking down hallways and up and down stairs. While he was talking I realized every room, every hallway, every section of the building had stories.

Eric showed me the room where, each Sunday morning before church services, the homeless gather to have coffee and breakfast. He told me that one of the biggest issues is the pets of the homeless and how to navigate allowing them to bring their best friends into the building. So they have an all-dogs-welcome policy, as long as they are friendly to others. I laughed as I told him this is an issue I've never had to discuss in a church staff meeting.

He walked me upstairs and showed me the counseling wing of their church. This was obviously a possible Sunday School wing, but instead, on one end was a section of offices where the church offers free counseling for individuals and couples, staffed by local university counseling interns and adminis-trated by their church staff. On the other end of the wing was a non-faith-based addiction recovery organization that works in partnership with them to serve the residents of the area. Imagine that, I thought silently: people who maybe don't believe in God working inside a church with people who do. And so, The Sanctuary's counseling office can exchange clients down the hall to meet with the addiction counselors, and they can be sent clients who sometimes need a more spiritual approach.

Eric walked me down the hall and told me about their merger with an older congregation that previously owned the building. He told a God story about how they met with him and asked if they could just give him the building. Eric initially wasn't looking for a building, just a room to rent in order to host a recovery meeting for the addicts in his new church. However, the older church was on the decline and wanted a vibrant congregation that was reaching the neighborhood to take their space. Instead of just taking over the building, The Sanctuary chose to merge with the other church, seeing value in the seniors retaining their voice and presence amongst a new community of worshipers.

We walked through the worship center of the church where weekly services are held. There were pews lining the room in the center, but along the side walls there were prayer and worship stations where people could interact with God in different ways: places to journal their hurts, to write out prayers for others, to create art during the service, to engage the Scriptures in fresh ways. There was a large cross up front with a luggage trunk at the base of it. Slips of paper were all around the cross so the worshipers could write down their own personal baggage: addiction, abuse, homelessness, loneliness, sins, hurts, and pain from life. These could be left in the trunk and exchanged for beautiful, hopeful words written out on small pages sitting in a basket on top of the trunk. Worshipers could leave their current baggage: *addict, broken, divorced,* and pick up a new identity: *loved, redeemed, forgiven, hopeful.*

Eric walked me downstairs to the basement and talked like a proud father about his community as he showed me the food pantry that feeds hundreds every week, and the clothing store for the students in the school next to them, where people can come and pick out donated, almost-new clothing for free.

With every turn of a corner, with every stairwell, there was a new story, a view of the kingdom of God at work. Each room spoke of life and you could visualize the people who came throughout the week. Rooms were not left unused, reserved for meetings, or Bible studies, though those could certainly happen, but the primary drive of this church and every space in it was to bring hope, healing, and a taste of the kingdom to people in Old Colorado City. The goal was not numerical growth: it was gospel, good news. As he talked, I could easily see that Eric's pride was not in "his" church, but in what God was doing through the church community he leads. From feeding the homeless in their building, to setting up community art projects in the nearby park, to working with local businesses to take care of the needy in their neighborhood, Eric and The Sanctuary community simply join God on mission.

One story Eric recounted particularly stood out to me. He talked about a woman who came to Christ one morning in their worship gathering. Eric approached her one day asking what brought her to a decision to follow Jesus. She talked about the first time she visited on a Sunday morning and smelled bacon and body odor mixed together near the room where the homeless were having breakfast. She went on to describe going into the bathroom and smelling vomit, where obviously someone had just gotten sick, a result of their binge the night before. Then, when she was in the worship gathering, the music started and she could tell that someone around her was carrying the smell of booze from drinking all night. "Then it hit me," she explained to him. "This place smells like my life, and I knew I would be safe."

If we're honest, all of us carry a little bit of smell in our life. It's not a smell we like, but it's the smell of reality, and of living, and it's the smell that Jesus often chose to hang out with. I don't know your particular or current circumstances, but if you're like me, I need the reminder that regularly using soap and toothpaste might just possibly cover up what's going on inside. The smell, or lack thereof, doesn't define our actual spiritual condition. Just because I smell like a fresh shower, doesn't mean I don't need some cleansing inside. Just because my breath doesn't smell like last night's bourbon doesn't mean I'm not numbing myself with some other addiction.

Let's be completely honest, we may be spit-shined on the outside, our lawn may be manicured, we may have the nicest car and clothes, but if people get close enough to us, there will be a smell of life on our breath. This is what the woman in Eric's church smelled that day. It wasn't hidden in the beauty of suburbia and the "I'm fine" responses of many church foyers. It was reality on the outside that reminded her of her need for the gospel on the inside. It was as if God was saying, "Don't say 'I'm fine' when asked how you are. Tell the truth and then come to me." This is the raw and unfiltered beauty of this church community. It ushers brokenness to the surface to meet face to face with a redeeming God.

At the beginning of every Sanctuary gathering, they welcome guests, and then read these words out loud:

> If you are a...
> Saint, Sinner, Loser, Winner, Abused, Abuser, Whore, Gambler, Lost, Fearful, ADHD, Liar, Hypocrite, Bastard, Lover, Cutter, Tweaker, Alcoholic, Adopted, Abandoned, Leftover, Divorced, LGBT, Alone, Old, Young, Driven, Cheater, Success, Infected, Rejected, Pierced, and Tattooed,
> Or just a Misfit...
> You are welcome here.

Eric will sometimes tell the story of this lady coming to Christ and then ask, "What does the gospel smell like to you?" This story and his follow-up question have been significant in my own view of the gospel and how it plays out in my engagement of others. It's a valid question and demands more than simply thinking about.

God gives an ever-present call to his *imago Dei*. It's the call to stop wandering and bring the smell and filth of life to him, so he can cleanse, redeem, and even change our smell into a different aroma. Though our past smells may haunt us in certain ways, God offers a new aroma to wear with our new identity in him. To this lady in Eric's church, the smell of raw reality made her feel safe, but being around other *imago Dei* who were transparent about their struggles didn't just leave her in that condition, of simply identifying with vomit and alcohol. The call was much greater. It was the call from the Holy Spirit to deeper places in her life, places she normally hid, and to bring those smells to the surface so she could be cleansed and given a new odor, a new identity. This is the offer to us as well, as people with smelly lives. Whether we wear our scent out in the open, or hide it underneath our presentable exterior, Jesus offers us the new smell of the gospel. It's a smell that redeems us and then goes with us into the places we live. The power of the new smell resides in the old smells underneath. It's not that all of our life is cleaned up in our behavior, but the power is in the new Jesus fragrance we wear, in spite of our past and present struggles.

Paul writes a statement to the church in Corinth, which talks about the way we smell to others:

> In the Messiah, in Christ, God leads us from place to place in one perpetual victory parade. Through us, he brings knowledge of Christ. Everywhere we go, people breathe in the exquisite fragrance. Because of Christ, we give off a sweet scent rising to God, which is

recognized by those on the way of salvation—
an aroma redolent with life.

2 CORINTHIANS 2:14–16

(MSG, italics mine)

Notice the italicized imagery of smelling like the kingdom. The point in this section of Paul's letter is significant. People will breathe in the fragrance of who we are, everywhere we go. And this fragrance is, "Because of Christ," not because of anything we do on our own. Many Christians can make the mistake of thinking that it's our religious and moral behavior or beliefs that give us a "sweet scent" to those we come in contact with. This is the exact opposite message of the gospel. It's not what we have experienced in our own relationship with Jesus, nor what we want to communicate to others. The power of the gospel is that our past failure and sins, and even current struggles, are given a new scent, but the scent is Jesus Christ, not us. On our own, we still carry the smell of dirt, if left apart from Christ's fragrance. The perpetual victory parade Paul speaks of is not a celebration of victory that we now can behave perfectly; rather it's the victory Jesus leads us in, giving us this new aroma.

Dust Cloud

One of my favorite cartoons growing up was, and still is, *Peanuts*.[36] Charlie Brown, Lucy, Snoopy and the gang are in

---

36 Charles M. Shulz, *Peanuts* comic strip.

many ways the illustrations of my life. I relate to the struggles of Charlie Brown, the ever-present "Psychiatric Help" lemonade stand with Lucy, and the thoughtful questions about life from Linus and Schroeder. My favorite character in the *Peanuts* clan is a boy nicknamed "Pig-Pen." I use his name in quotes because that's how it has always been written in the comic strip. We never really learn his real name but are told his nickname, by him, in 1954 when he first appears. The thing you notice about "Pig-Pen" is that everywhere he goes, he carries a cloud of dust around him. Every time he moves it seems to invite a bigger dust cloud. There are a few times when "Pig-Pen" gets clean, but only for a short time. Invariably, the dust cloud returns, and everywhere he walks, and in everything he does, he is surrounded by a cloud of dust that labels him with his name. No one wonders who "Pig-Pen" is. It's evident as soon as he enters the room. The cloud, the dirt, the smell tell you it's him.

I can remember my teen years. They were mostly happy and exciting, but I made a lot of mistakes. These were years when I struggled in my relationship with my parents. I seemed to make wrong decisions almost weekly. I remember feeling like I often carried a dust cloud around with me. I gained a notorious reputation, known for skipping school, or running away from home, or just always living on the edge. From twelve years old to twenty-two I felt like I was constantly running from my dust cloud, trying to wash it away with a new success or direction in life. If we're honest with ourselves, many of us feel and live the same way. Even as we grow older we can still be running from dust clouds because we feel labeled by them. It can be embarrassing for people to know us by our mistakes, our past journeys, our less than perfect seasons of life. To make our dust clouds seem smaller, we can fall into the trap of judging other people by their cloud of dust. Like "Pig-Pen" they just walk into our life and bring a cloud of dusty living behind them. We're programed to automatically filter dust out like a vacuum, so we avoid dusty people, "Pig-Pens." However, our call is not to avoid dust. Rather, we want to engage the dust of people's lives and introduce them to the new scent we have in Christ. We want to invite them into the victory parade with us, following Jesus, along with multitudes of dusty people who now smell good. Our message, from one dust cloud to another should be, "Come, join the parade!"

Gratefully, when we give over our lives to Jesus and begin following him, we are given a new name and a new identity: *child of God, Christ-follower, disciple, Jesus person.* I was always taught in church that I was washed clean by "accepting Jesus into my heart." While I understood and embraced the theology behind this statement, as life with Jesus went on, I realized the dust clouds still followed me a bit. For me, it wasn't that Jesus washed away the past clouds of dust, but he gave me a new identity in spite of the fact that the past still followed me wherever I walked. He gave me a new name—not *"Pig-Pen"* but *Co-Heir of the kingdom.*[37] Not only is everything in

---

37 Romans 8:17.

the kingdom that is his, also mine, but he also gave me a new smell, a "sweet scent." It's puzzling to people when they see us walking as Christ-followers, in the identity of Jesus, but still transparent about our dust cloud. It's a powerful demonstration of God and his grace in our life. By all appearances, we should be labeled "Pig-Pen," wandering and dusty. Instead, we walk through life like it's a victory parade, and Jesus is at the front of the line giving us a new fragrance and identity in him, in spite of the dust around us.

Even Paul acknowledged his dust clouds. In Acts 22 Paul tells of how he used to kill and beat Christians, dragging them from places of worship and putting them in chains, but then Jesus showed up and called him to follow. Paul carried this dust cloud of being a hunter of those who followed the same Jesus he now did. We are even told how Paul tried to join the group of disciples right after his conversion, but they were afraid of him, aware of his former life and his persecution of Christians.[38] Wow, talk about a dust cloud when you walk in the room. However, Paul carried a different scent after Jesus, a new identity. In fact, God used him to write much of the New Testament and also to plant numerous churches throughout the Mediterranean area! The church you are now part of was multiplied and spread through the work of a guy who was known as a killer of Christians, but given a new identity and scent in Jesus Christ.

It is a life lived out loud when we walk around with our

38 Acts 9:26-27.

dust clouds showing, allowing God to show his power through our failures and shortcomings. "Pig-Pen" never cared what everyone else thought but just lived into who he was. As Christians we often do the opposite: we try to hide our cloud. But consider the message we communicate to other dusty people when we openly acknowledge our own failures and tell them about a God who loves them in spite of the dust. He is a God who breathed life into dust to create them, and offers to breathe life into them again with the redeeming scent of Jesus Christ. Yes, walking into a room with a dust cloud means people might talk, they might ask questions, they might even judge you, but in the end, you get to be a visible example of the aroma of the kingdom. It will be curious and winsome to people when you smell like the gospel in the midst of the smell of life. It may be a bit like mixing bacon and body odor. Through your example, those around you may understand the depth of God's grace and how his invitation is for those who smell like dust. Just maybe, when they see you now, they will respond, "That smells like I want my life to smell."

The Big Cover-Up

Kitty and I are blessed with four children and they are all fantastic humans. We still can't believe we've raised such cool kids! Our oldest two are boys, and the senior of the bunch is our son Carson. He is one of the joys of our life—a fantastic worship leader, a great husband to his wife, Corrie, and an authentic Christ-follower. Carson was a pretty typical middle and high schooler. He went through the normal growing pains of teenage boys, many things I myself journeyed through. We often joke that Carson, through no fault of his own, grew up in the "age of Axe." This was a few-year period when there was a new men's cologne company that made body sprays, shower gel, and colognes.

Axe quickly became the rage among teen boys when it first came out. The average boy, including Carson, figured out very quickly that they could use half a can of Axe spray instead of taking a shower. In reality, you smelled fairly good, and the scent stayed with you for a long time. It didn't matter that other people in the house couldn't enter the bathroom for about four hours following its use, the end result was worth it. Carson, and millions of other teens around the country, smelled like Axe, and you could sense the growth and evangelism happening in the "church of Axe." Parents around the country were taken by surprise, many simply living with the intensity of the smell, since it was better than fighting over showers.

Today it feels like we often cover up our own lives in a type of religious Axe spray. We have a tendency to think that following Jesus means we will live a perfectly well-behaved life that doesn't break the rules of Scripture. Our inability to carry out that kind of religion means we not only live with a constant sense of failure, but it also masks the gospel from the rest of the world. Instead, the activity of church membership, attendance, and biblical knowledge often serves to create a smell around us that the world senses, but isn't attracted to. It's not a "sweet smell" but a religious one. In error, we often find ourselves trading the sweet smell of Jesus for the smell of religion. This was what the Pharisees did: they used Axe. They boiled down the essence of what being a person of God was, and instead measured that life in terms of religious activity and conduct, rather than a heart transformed by God.[39]

When we measure our Christianity by our behaviors and church attendance, it's akin to using half a can of Axe spray. We smell like a Christian for a time, but it's more like a cover-up. To make it worse, if religious activity becomes the foundation of our identity with God, we miss the whole calling to follow Jesus. Our true scent is found in the fact that Jesus came for us, we gave him our whole life, and now we follow and live the life of a restored dust cloud. This restoration comes *not* from the activity of following, but as a gift from the One we follow. If you come across someone who is really more impressed with your biblical knowledge or postures than the way you live your life, then just take a whiff and you'll probably pick up the scent of Axe on them. Underneath the cover-up is the same person you are, with the same challenges in life. The invitation is the same for all of us; don't cover up with the smell of religion to mask your struggles. Allow the cloud to be a transparent piece of your life, but let the fragrance of Jesus give you the scent of the kingdom of God.

When it comes down to it, we have to decide for ourselves what the smell of the gospel is like. Is good news just about crossing a line of salvation, or is it about a God who welcomes

39 E.g., see Luke 11:37–54.

us into a room with our dust cloud following us, along with the smell of life's body odor? Is good news simply about attendance at a church building or is it about God attending to our mess with forgiveness, grace, mercy, and his breath? Ultimately, whatever we define the smell of the gospel to be will be the smell we carry with us. If we focus our life on religion, then religion is the smell we will carry into the world. If we smell like brokenness, redeemed and restored, walking with the cloud of dust but breathed on by God, then we will be seen and smelled for who we are: a regular broken person, but with the sweet smell of Christ around us.

When we come to grips with our own dust cloud, then we can easily see and accept other people in spite of theirs. It's strange how a change in perspective about our own redeemed life in Jesus can change how we view others. Everyone we come in contact with has a little bit of "Pig-Pen" in their life, but many times it's just covered up with another scent. This is why churches like The Sanctuary are so amazing. They make us feel normal, because our normal broken self is invited to be there in the community and in the presence of God. The true message of grace is that God invites us into a life where dust clouds aren't scary—they're reality. He invites us to put away the religion that covers up the journey of life, and instead bring people and their dust clouds to him, to capture his breath. We are invited by God into an amazing work of restoring people's lives, introducing them to a God who heals, repairs, and gives new purpose, the God who says, "Join the parade."

Ironically, you will find your own loud life when you leave the Axe of religious events and calendars and engage other people who carry dust clouds like we do. It's in those places, usually outside the walls of the church, where we find out that God will begin using our stories in amazing ways. The dust clouds we try to hide become the examples of God's grace and forgiveness, the power behind our story. Other dust cloud carriers begin to see that they too can be loved and forgiven by the Jesus who walked dusty roads and loved dusty people. When we begin to activate our Bible knowledge by loving our neighbor, we find a whole new world of Christianity. It doesn't smell like church, or Bible studies…it doesn't smell like Axe. Being a Christian should smell like Jesus himself. Yes, we can smell like Jesus, look like Jesus and live the same ministry he did. That's what he's wanted all along, for us to follow him, our dust and all, on dusty roads.

ONE LOUDER STEP

Journal about the dust cloud you now carry, but may hide from others. Be honest about your past, and maybe current, pains and trials. How can you be respectfully transparent to others about your own struggles, while carrying the new scent of Christ in your life?

6

Will's Eyes

We were about six months from opening Third Space Coffee and decided to rent a co-working space to throw a preview party. Invitations were sent to eighty close friends and family to gather with us and come taste coffee and sugar waffles, purchase street art for a charity, listen to music from our good friend Chuck, and catch a little bit of the vision for our new venture.

I had four of our future baristas there that night, doing pour-overs of some of the best single origin coffee. One of those baristas was my son Will. The room was packed with people having a great time, the music was dynamic, and the sidewalk where I was standing most of the night was packed with people. All of a sudden, Will, who was behind the counter serving coffee, came running through the crowd toward the front door, a cup of coffee in one hand and a waffle in the other. My immediate thought was that Will was going to have a messy accident with one of our guests, so I moved toward the door to intercept him. After taking about four steps, I stopped as I saw him running down the sidewalk away from the crowd, and toward a lone figure walking slowly away from us with a heavy pack.

Will was chasing down a homeless man who had walked completely unnoticed through our presence on the sidewalk. As I watched Will help this man take off his pack and sit down against the building wall, handing over the cup and plate, I heard him say, "Here, dude, this is for you." ("Dude," by the way, is Will's word of affection for another person.)

How had Will even noticed this man in the bustle of the room full of guests and loud music? The line was backed up at the coffee bar, and the baristas could hardly keep up with the demand, but Will had looked through the window and seen this crouched-over human make his way through our celebration to get on with his life walking down the street. In his love for others, Will wanted to make sure this man knew that he was seen, and so he took the time to let him know.

Seeing Will help another person didn't surprise me. God has wired him naturally that way, but I learned something that night about myself. I learned that, as a pastor, I didn't necessarily notice people the way I should. I was surprised that this homeless man made it past without me or my other guests noticing, many of us being in some form of ministry. To this day, when I think of Will's act of love, I think of Jesus' words when he's talking to the disciples about what entering the kingdom of God will look like. He gives the metaphor of a shepherd dividing a flock into sheep and goats: those who have lived as announcers of the kingdom on earth, and those who have not. He explains to them:

> "'Enter, you who are blessed by my Father! Take what's coming to you in this kingdom. It's been ready for you since the world's foundation. And here's why:
> I was hungry and you fed me,
> I was thirsty and you gave me a drink,
> I was homeless and you gave me a room,
> I was shivering and you gave me clothes,
> I was sick and you stopped to visit,
> I was in prison and you came to me.'
> Then those 'sheep' are going to say, 'Master, what are you talking about? When did we ever see you hungry and feed you, thirsty and give you a drink? And when did we ever see you sick or in prison and come to you?' Then the King will say, 'I'm telling the solemn truth: Whenever you did one of these things to someone overlooked or ignored, that was me—you did it to me.'"
>
> MATTHEW 25:34–40 (MSG)

Many people read this passage of Scripture and interpret it as a litmus test for who makes it into heaven and who doesn't, but what if we alternatively read it with the heart of Jesus?

Rather than trying to figure out what will get us over the line and into heaven, what if we saw it instead as an invitation to participate in the kingdom of God? Jesus starts a list of things we might do to participate with him: feed the poor, give a drink to the thirsty, visit those who are sick. But this list is likely not exhaustive: it's Jesus' way of prompting us to imagine the ways we might notice the person who walked right past us and give them some hope and attention. It's the invitation to open our eyes and see fellow humans.

Will was an example to me of choosing not to overlook the least and the ignored who are right in front of us. In fact, based on Jesus' words in Matthew, Will illustrates to us all that when he chased this man down to show some kindness, he was actually chasing down Jesus and loving him. His act of love for a homeless man was an act of love toward his Savior.

We often forget to look right in front of our faces for the ways in which God wants us to live out the kingdom, bringing a taste of that kingdom to the streets. That night, it tasted like a waffle, a cup of coffee, and some love from a teenage boy who noticed an old homeless man. Now I do realize the tensions with trying to feed and help all the homeless we come in sight of. I recognize it's costly to help everyone we see that is in need. I don't have all those answers, and I don't pretend to know exactly how you should respond. What seems fairly clear though, is that we show our love for Jesus when we show our love for the forgotten and overlooked, for those in need.

A person doesn't have to be physically homeless or poor

to feel overlooked or in need. At our coffee shop we sometimes see homelessness happening around our café tables. At
any one time, we might have fifty people in Third Space all
talking and meeting for various reasons. Sometimes it's a business meeting, sometimes a casual gathering. Once in a while
we witness tears and pain as one person is sharing something
with another. We can tell when life is heavy at certain tables
as we see two or three people praying together, sometimes
clutching a tissue, or we might notice it in the furrowed brow
on people's faces as they come to the register. I've told all my
employees to brighten someone's day whenever needed. They
have the freedom to buy someone their coffee, and the staff all
aspire to help people not only feel wanted, but honored, in our
space. This policy started one day when a single mom walked
into Third Space with four kids in tow. She was visibly already
worn down, but when she realized she'd forgotten her wallet, it
drove her to tears. One of my employees called me and told me
the situation. I told them to make her whatever she wanted,
coffee and food, and we'd foot the bill. After that incident,
she reached out to me and told me how that one act totally
changed her perspective for the day. Sometimes the person
who can afford the five-dollar latte and nine-dollar quiche
feels a little poor in their life and hungry for something more.
This policy in our shop is a way of honoring what Will taught
me that one night, to use coffee as a tool to say, "We see you
and we love you."

The Homeless Next Door

Often those who feel the most homeless may be the ones who live in the house next door to us. They may have a roof over their head, but perhaps because of a broken relationship, or other life issues, they don't feel at home. Life may be presenting circumstances where they thirst for hope and purpose, and hunger to be seen. Right there in your neighborhood, apartment complex, workplace, gym, or your own favorite coffee shop, I guarantee you there are homeless people right in front of your eyes. They are wearing business suits, smart jeans, and smiles on their faces, but deep inside they feel homeless.

It's up to each one of us to be intentional with people around us, joining God in the ways he is already at work in their lives. We already live in places where we can lean into another person's life: the kids' soccer field, the exercise class, the workplace, our neighborhood street. While it's important to find a place in our life to engage with the marginalized, it's almost mandatory that we develop eyes to see the people around us who appear to have life under control. We can't just let them walk through the crowd unnoticed. We need to have Will's eyes, those that notice a person to love and connect with. Eyes that see other people, accompanied with actions that communicate, "I see you."

Kitty and I were caught off guard the first time our son Will brought a strange kid home needing a place to sleep. Adam was a teenager who Will met at the skate park and, after a few days, Will figured out he was sleeping in the park. Will, being the human that he is, brought Adam home with him. I still remember hearing Will thump his footsteps upstairs from our basement and round the corner, then in a whisper saying, "Mom and Dad, this kid Adam is downstairs and he's been sleeping outside. We can't just let him sleep outside—it's too cold." His heart just couldn't bear the pain of someone sleeping alone in the cold of Colorado. Maybe a little nervous, but submitting to Will's instincts, we told him Adam could sleep on the couch downstairs. This was to be the first of many similar experiences.

Instead of stray dogs or cats, Will would bring home teenagers. Monument, the area we live in, consists of nice houses, nice cars, manicured lawns, home-owner associations, and either upwardly mobile or safely retired residents. It is not the area of town you'd expect to find the physically homeless. What Will discovered was a consistent problem in our area of teenage kids being kicked out of their homes either as punishment or as leverage to enforce better behavior. It was a complete shock to Kitty and me when we found out this was going on right under our noses, and in more than one instance. Sure, we understand the tensions of having teenagers and trying to find a balance of letting them live their own life but also helping them make good choices. What we couldn't understand was kicking them out into the night air to fend for themselves, make their own way, and in one case, even finish high school on their own. We came across a dozen stories like this, with many of these kids hurting on the inside from being turned away by their parents. At our house they found a sofa to sleep on and some warm meals. In some cases they found surrogate parents in us. Will told his mom during this time, "You know, Mom, when you die, there are going to be a lot of people at your funeral." A bit shocked at the strange wording of this compliment, she understood he was verbalizing his appreciation of her loving his friends well.

Anyone coming home from Colorado Springs or Denver and driving back to our neighborhood would never have imagined there were homeless teens in our community. They just wouldn't notice them, because we can so easily drive up to our houses, open the garage, drive in and shut the door behind us. It's easy to keep your head down and fail to notice people in our community; to not see people. What Kitty and I grew to realize and understand with each of these encounters was that the beautiful houses around us were, in many cases, actually broken inside. While the housing structures were above average, the relational structures inside were often way below. There were deep social hurts going on around us all the time that were not easily seen. For every kid we could see on our couch, there were likely several more we couldn't see. From talking with these teens we learned that they came from complex family situations, sometimes involving drug issues with a parent, marital breakdowns or physical abuse. While sprinkler systems kept lawns looking their best, the lives inside many homes were broken and dying of thirst.

I am convinced there are families and homes like this

within your eyesight as well. The homeless are all around us. They exist within sight of our back deck and over the fence as we all mow lawns and play with the dog. They exist down the apartment hallway, or in the work cubicle next to you. You will find them if you just take notice. Lift your head, put down your phone, take out the ear buds, look people in the face, go into your neighborhood searching. Walk your neighborhood streets, looking to meet people and hear their story. It may take time, but you will eventually find them. Noticing those who feel detached and wandering takes intentionality. It requires looking them in the eye, learning their names, finding common points of contact, gathering around a BBQ grill… it takes stopping and noticing their pain and needs. You may just find them where you least expect to: the homeless in the homes around you.

Walking the "Right" Side of the Road

There's a story in the Bible that Jesus tells to illustrate this point of noticing other people. We call this parable "The Good Samaritan," and it's told to countless children in Sunday Schools, and then occasionally to adults in a Sunday morning sermon. The story is given by Jesus at the prodding of a religious man who wants to quiz Jesus on the Old Testament statement to "love your neighbor."[40] After the man asks (I imagine in a sarcastic tone), "So who is my neighbor?" Jesus responds:

---

40 Leviticus 19:18.

"There was once a man traveling from Jerusalem to Jericho. On the way he was attacked by
robbers. They took his clothes, beat him up, and
went off leaving him half-dead. Luckily, a priest
was on his way down the same road, but when
he saw him he angled across to the other side.
Then a Levite religious man showed up; he also
avoided the injured man. A Samaritan traveling
the road came on him. When he saw the man's
condition, his heart went out to him. He gave
him first aid, disinfecting and bandaging his
wounds. Then he lifted him onto his donkey,
led him to an inn, and made him comfortable.
In the morning he took out two silver coins and
gave them to the innkeeper, saying, 'Take good
care of him. If it costs any more, put it on my
bill—I'll pay you on my way back.'
"What do you think? Which of the three became
a neighbor to the man attacked by robbers?"
"The one who treated him kindly," the religion
scholar responded.
Jesus said, "Go and do the same."

LUKE 10:30–37 (MSG)

In American culture, the words Levite, priest and Samaritan
don't hold much meaning to us (short of us knowing about
Catholic priests). But to Jesus' original listeners, it was a
paradigm-shifting illustration. As I mentioned in chapter one,

Jews looked down upon Samaritans. They were half-breeds of Jewish society and worshiped God in a different way, and a different place.[41] They even believed some different things about God, mixing traditional Jewish worship with other religions. In the story, Jesus draws attention to the priest and Levite "luckily" coming upon the situation but then passing by the injured man—the people considered most religious were the ones who failed to take action and bring the kingdom to bear in a moment of need. You can visualize them both going to the side of the road to pass by the lifeless-looking figure lying there. The person who *did* notice, the half-breed and hated Samaritan (with so-called wrong theology), stopped and showed practical kindness and love to this man in need. Jesus' shocking point was that the Samaritan was actually following the instructions of God in Scripture more so than the two religious men. The priest and the Levite, in wanting to stay ceremonially clean and avoid encountering blood or death, were focused on the rules of their religion. The Samaritan noticed someone who was unnoticed and in need. And so, this fictional Samaritan, and my son Will, shared the same eyesight. Those listening to the story would have been convinced that the priest and Levite were closer to God because they followed the religious rules, but the Samaritan becomes the hero of the story, and God's very hands and feet in loving his neighbor! Before we're too quick to judge the priest and the Levite, let's remember we can be just the same in our everyday lives. What kinds of people

41 John 4:19–20.

do we feel might pollute our holiness or purity by sharing life with them?

My experience is that there are many people lying on the side of the road beat up by life in various ways. Many of these people are on the very streets where we live and are occupying the houses to the right and left of us. As you drive home one day, start counting how many front doors you pass on the way to your own house or apartment. Whatever number you end up with, that's how many stories are waiting for you to notice them. Noticing, however, requires our intentionality.

If you're like me, you've spent most of your life and still spend most of your days getting from one appointment or place to the next, and usually we're doing it at light speed. Our lives are often driven by our calendar, and so we rush down the road to the next thing on our list. I hit a point where I realized I had my head down too much in life, focused on my own schedule. I never even stopped to wonder who was in the house at the end of the block. At the grocery, I would just hurry down the aisle, not really noticing who was in my way, never making eye contact, or looking for small talk. I always fiddled with my wallet in the checkout line, or worse, my phone, as if to communicate to the person helping me, "Please don't bother me...just check out my purchase, please." Oh, I'd leave with a smile and a "Have a nice day," but the reality was, I just wanted to walk on the other side of the road. We all need to walk on the "right" side, the side that encounters people in need. We all need the eyes of the Samaritan, and of Will.

The Eyes of God

My wife, Kitty, has some fantastic insights about Scripture and the stories that are illustrated in the Bible. One of her favorites, one she has told to countless people and to our children, is the story of Hagar. In Genesis 16 we're told of this woman, who is the slave of Sarai, Abram's wife. Abram and Sarai have not been able to conceive a child who would be Abram's heir, so Sarai tells her husband to sleep with her slave in order to have a child. (I don't think Kitty would ever suggest this to me.)

Abram and Hagar have a child, and then as you can imagine, jealousy takes over and Sarai and Hagar begin to have bad feelings about each other. Sarai starts to mistreat Hagar because of the child she conceived, which is of course Abram's. Hagar, in her pain and confusion, packs her meager belongings and her newborn and runs from the situation, eventually finding herself at a spring of water in the desert. We're told an angel of the Lord appears to her as she sits there. It's not hard to envision Hagar sitting with her child, probably under whatever shade they can find from a tree or bush, wondering why life has dealt them these circumstances.

The angel and Hagar have a conversation about her plight and her plan to run from her mistress. Then the angel surprises Hagar by instructing her to go back and submit to Sarai but also gives her a glimpse into the plan God has for her life. The child she is carrying is going to be the father of a nation, a key piece of what God wants to do in the world.

Hagar, sitting by the spring with her baby, alone, homeless, with no identity left, beaten up by life, immediately sees her importance in God's plan. She is given the vision to see that the pain in her life can lead to some amazing involvement in the kingdom of God. The uncomfortable circumstances of being a slave to Sarai are minimized in the breadth of her place in God's plan. With her eyes opened and her hope returned, at that crossroads in life she names God, *El Roi*, "the God who sees me."[42] At a time when she felt unseen and unwanted, as a slave of Sarai and used by Abram, she was chased, found, and given a purpose by the God who sees her.

Thinking of my own journey with God, it amazes me that not only do I now realize God sees me, but I have the ability to bring this same hope and vision to others. When I take the time to notice other people in their moments of need, in the places where life dishes out trials, it's like I'm saying, "I see you." As a Christ-follower, sent by Jesus to engage the neighbor who is having a hard time, I also communicate to them that God sees them.

As we encounter people in our neighborhood, at work, at the grocery checkout, the coffee shop, we have the opportunity to say, through our actions and intent, that they are seen by God. We may not know the "side of the road" circumstances weighing on them at that point; we may not see why they are crouched in the shade by a spring, but we have the chance to connect with them and let them know they are seen. When we live incarnational and missional lives, in intentional ways,

42 Genesis 16:13.

and see another person, we can be God's agent. We join him in mission and communicate, through our own actions of being sent, that God sees them. Remember Jesus' words, "whatever you did for one of the least of these…"(Matthew 25:40). And so, seeing another human, an *imago Dei*, and noticing them is not trivial and insignificant. Helping someone in need is not simply social justice, separated from faith. This kind of eyesight, where we notice those crouched by the spring, lying on the side of the road, weaving their way through the crowd unnoticed, is actually living out the kingdom of God, and it's loving Jesus himself when we stop and notice them. It's bringing the kingdom to bear in a world that beats up people and leaves them on the side of the road. Noticing people is like taking the time to run down the sidewalk and sit someone down with a waffle and hot cup of coffee and say, "Here, dude, I see you."

Chased, Sought, and Adopted

When the gospel engulfs a person's life, it's God saying, "I see you, and you're my child." This is the greatest gift we can give other people: to let someone know their Father is seeking them out and sees them, their life, their struggles, their brokenness, their pain. It is perhaps the message they need at that very moment. To be adopted into the family of God becomes their path to belonging and healing.

Sharing the gospel with people is about letting them know they are seen, seen by a God who loves them, and seen by his kingdom people. The most tangible lesson I ever learned about the gospel happened when we adopted our youngest daughter, Jia. She is exquisite in beauty and smart as a whip. Though she was born in China, we don't really think of her as Asian, or adopted anymore. She's just part of our family. In fact, you can ask my wife how many times she's given birth, and she'll probably say, "Four," because of our four children.

We had the excitement of taking a trip to China with all our children to retrace Jia's early life journey. We found her hometown, her neighborhood, and the orphanage she started life in. We even found her early foster family and had dinner with them one night. What was surreal to me was that the story seemed so very foreign. Jia is my daughter, my child, and I don't remember being a father apart from her. I wouldn't be who I am without her.

Adoption is perhaps the greatest example of being seen and accepted as a child. Theologian J. I. Packer writes,

> If you want to judge how well a person understands Christianity, find out how much he makes of the thought of being God's child, and having God as his Father. If this is not the thought that prompts and controls his worship and prayers and his whole outlook on life, it means that he does not understand Christianity very well at all.[. . .]"Father" is the Christian name for God. [43]

---

43 J.I. Packer, *Knowing God* (Downer's Grove: IVP, 1973), 201–202.

Adoption is a key and critical message of the gospel. Adoption implies that a parent goes to find and invite a child to be their own. Paul reminds the church in Galatia that Jesus was sent in order to adopt: "God sent his Son, born of a woman, born under the law, to redeem those under the law, that we might receive adoption to sonship"(Galatians 4:4–5). However, it seems that much more emphasis has been placed on *people coming to find God*. When we present to culture an invitation to come to us, to come and join the family (join the church), we don't always give this picture of the Father seeking his children. God relentlessly pursues us: he has come to *seek* and save the lost.[44] He is the Father who doesn't just stand and wait for the prodigal son to walk the whole length of the road to him. *He runs toward him.*[45] The prophet Ezekiel also speaks of God's heart: "I will seek the lost, bring back the scattered, bind up the broken and strengthen the sick" (Ezekiel 34:16 NASB). Of course, an individual has to make a personal decision to follow Jesus. However, we must give equal weight and voice to the fact that the Father is actively seeking all of us. When we look at other *imago Dei*, we must realize that God is looking for them also, calling to them, just as he is to you and to me. Their value as children is equal to ours.

Jia's adoption started with us going to find her and then saying, "We see you, we love you, come and be with us." The message of adoption should be our key tool in evangelism. The

44 Luke 19:10.
45 Luke 15:20.

invitation to be seen and be loved, to belong and to be known, is stronger, more compelling and more credible than the steps to becoming a church member or crossing some line of salvation. Our message is not that a person must come and find God, but that God has already found them and wants to call them "child."

Though it happens occasionally, it's becoming increasingly rare for people to come to the church building to see if they can be adopted. We, the "sent" people of Jesus, are the ones who get to hit the streets and spread the adoption message. We get to live a life that invites others to become siblings in a family in which they are seen and known.

When we make it a habit to use our peripheral vision in our daily comings and goings, we will start to notice people on the side of the road like the Samaritan did. It's weird—they will just start coming into focus like ghosts that were there all along. We will, all of a sudden, begin noticing the ways we can stop for the thirsty, feed the hungry, give hope to those in pain. We start seeing people for who they are. We feel pain with them, we thirst with them, we strive for a better world with them. Our stories may look different, but our goals are the same…we all want to be seen, we all want to be loved.

ONE LOUDER STEP

As you go through your day, begin looking for people you don't normally see or notice. Stop and talk to them if possible. Ask about their life, what they do, how long they've lived in your city. If poor or homeless, buy them a cup of coffee and stop to find out a little about their story. Put on Will's eyes and see them!

7

Splinters

I have a tendency to get splinters. I am a proud do-it-your-selfer and like to work on anything that needs fixing. My dad raised me to be a firm believer that I can accomplish anything as long as I'm willing to learn how to do it. With me this usually includes Google and a little trial and error. Last year I built new stair railings, acquiring several splinters in the process. I work on vintage cars and love to spend my time fashioning and restoring metal and wood back to its former glory. As a result, splinters live in my fingers...metal, wood, fiberglass... small fragments broken off from the larger piece. My thumbnail has become an expert at digging on splinters in my fingertips until they let loose and work their way out.

Ironically, one of my childhood fears was getting splinters, and I remember the birth of this fear. Ten years old each, my friend Randall and I were riding minibikes in the pecan orchard at his house in Arkansas. (Minibikes were small motorcycle-like contraptions that used lawnmower engines, usually found at a place like a small-town hardware store.) We went roaring across the harvested soybean field next to their orchard toward the wooded area on the other side. Dust was flying, and we were laughing and yelling at the top of our lungs, pretending to be Evel Knievel, tempting fate and certain death. As we approached the dirt mound on the side of the field it seemed entirely reasonable to jump it at full speed, even though we couldn't see over the five-foot grass on the other side. I mean, at ten years old and with motorcycles (well, minibikes), what could possibly hurt us? Our landing would surely be met by the solid ground leading into the woodland. Randall was ahead of me and hit the dirt mound with skill and style. After all, it was his field and his minibikes. He cleared what we couldn't see as we approached the dirt mound: the old, rolled up, rusty barbed wire fence. I didn't see it. The last thing I remember was the jolt in my body from hitting that mound of dirt, causing my helmet to go forward and over my face. I didn't see where I landed…in the middle of the barbed wire and fence railings that had been piled up for years. Besides finding a split in my leg that took about twenty stitches (though I usually say forty for effect), the fence post attached to the barbed wire left a huge eight-inch splinter in my leg that had to be removed with what was in my mind *major* surgery. I remember the tetanus shots and the digging required to get it out. While I'm sure now that it was very light surgery, my memory is of amputation. From that point on, splinters frightened me.

As I've grown older, my fear of splinters has shifted to an expectancy of carrying them, sometimes multiple ones at a time. Splinters are a natural consequence of the things I enjoy. If I want to work on vintage cars, metal splinters will be a necessary part of that identity. If I want to stretch myself as a DIY homeowner, then splinters will come with each project. Splinters are the proof of the hobbies and work that fill my spare time. They are markers of the identity I want to carry.

Carrying a Cross

In the Gospel of Luke, Jesus is praying with his disciples and tells them:

> "Whoever wants to be my disciple must deny themselves and take up their cross daily and follow me. For whoever wants to save their life will lose it, but whoever loses their life for me will save it."
>
> LUKE 9:23–24

It occurs to me that a person following Jesus might expect to get splinters. Carrying a huge piece of wood every day would certainly leave behind slivers of wood in a person's hand and shoulder, markers of their focus and what they spent their time doing. Of course, Jesus wasn't proposing that this band of disciples carry around twelve big crosses of wood everywhere they went.

Jesus makes the point in this teaching that anyone who wants to follow him must deny their own comforts, goals, and even their safety to do so. This is incredibly difficult, especially in our society, which is built on self-focus and self-reliance. A large bank account and a big house are the defining markers of success, and so denying ourselves doesn't fit neatly in contemporary culture. Denying ourselves can leave us open to being hurt or injured. It can leave us open to splinters.

As incarnational missionaries in the places we live, work, and play, we need to live lives of integrity, where our story flows out of the way we live. This is our life out loud. Frost and Hirsch remind us that, "We are our messages"—our life shows our true identity.[46] It is impossible to maintain integrity when we assent to one belief but live another way. In other words, our splinters exhibit how we spend our time. We can't say we carry a cross but never get splinters.

Carrying a Cross Is Risky

One of the hardest times in life for Kitty and me happened just after our move to Monument, Colorado. I was on staff at a church, and Kitty and I were introduced to a family who lived across the interstate from us. They lived in an apartment in a section of town where people were typically living week to week, struggling to make ends meet. After meeting them through some strange circumstances, we decided to take this

---

46 Michael Frost and Alan Hirsch, *The Shaping of Things to Come* (Grand Rapids: Baker Books, 2003), 192–195.

family a meal and reach out, to be the love of Christ to them. Their lives were far from Jesus, and they sometimes used drugs to help them cope with their day-to-day hardship. Living in their apartment was a single mom, Linda, her three daughters, one of her daughter's boyfriend, and another young woman, Rachel.

As we got to know this family, Kitty regularly spent time with the mom, Linda, hoping to be a light in her life, trying to point her away from the decisions that were regularly pulling her down. Through meals, time together, praying, and talking, we all became connected with this family. Linda even decided to come off drugs at one point and ended up spending Christmas Eve at our house detoxing. While I was leading worship for church services, Kitty remembers spending Christmas Eve with Linda over the toilet in our house, trying to help her overcome her addiction.

Rachel, the young eighteen-year-old woman living with Linda, was openly gay. It didn't really bother us that she was gay, but it wasn't something we had encountered much in our secluded church circles of the past. We took it all in stride, loved her the same as anyone else, and it helped us learn to practice the lesson of seeing people as people first, something we already believed.

While Rachel's sexual orientation was easy to get used to, her rough and belligerent attitude was a challenge. She liked to display a tough exterior and was very defiant of society and authority. She was a drug user and had a hard time keeping a job. Linda's living room served as Rachel's bedroom, and so she seemed to be a little like a squatter. But Linda was support-ive of her and she was part of their tribe, so we accepted her as well, and loved her the best we could.

Kitty's love and concern pierced through Rachel's tough exterior, and Kitty started finding times where she could speak into her life, giving her wisdom and guidance to help her make better long-term decisions. As Kitty kept loving Rachel, she began spending a lot of time at our house. Rachel became really good friends with our oldest daughter, also named Kitty (we'll call her LK, "Little Kitty," a pet name many of us have given to her). They spent a lot of time watching TV and hang-ing out at our house. LK was fifteen at the time and Rachel was eighteen, but they seemed to have some things in common, and we were glad Rachel was finding community with us.

The day came when LK informed us that she and Rachel were dating and in a relationship. She expressed that she had hidden, and wrestled with, long-held feelings around her own sexual orientation. The relationship with Rachel seemed to be the trigger for Kitty to finally bring her feelings into the open with us.

I have to be completely honest and tell you that, while my wife and I are far from homophobic and judgmental of sexual orientations, it was unfamiliar territory for us to journey with one of our children. It took us a little by surprise and took several days to digest. It wasn't that we were disappointed in who she was as a person as much as it was a very new thing for us to experience in our family's identity. We believed, and still do, that our theology is ours to hold, and that God will communicate with others about their own theology and beliefs. We can certainly have discussions about what we believe with anyone, but we're not going to beat people up with what we think the Bible says about a particular topic. However, this became much harder when it was our minor daughter with an adult woman who seemed to make very poor life decisions. On the one hand we were working through a new picture of LK's sexual orientation and simply loving her for the person she is. On the other hand we were not very comfortable with the person she decided to date for the first time, not to mention LK was still a minor.

The splinter sunk deep, deeper than the minibike accident. I found myself with tunnel-vision, and all of life seemed to be out of focus except for this one thing. My little girl was having a relationship with an older woman who was not exactly living a stable life. I controlled my anger, mostly, though I didn't react perfectly, and there are several things I did and said that I wish could be replayed in a different way now. I dug at the splinter, but it just wouldn't come out.

We did all we could to protect LK and keep things as healthy as possible, establishing boundaries around their relationship. They weren't allowed to leave the house alone, but we allowed Rachel to come to us and they could watch movies and hang out. To shut down the relationship would have been counterproductive, not to mention that we've always tried to help our kids make their own decisions, rather than making decisions for them. We feared LK might leave home and lose her trust in us. Trust is incredibly valuable in the relational economy we have with our children. At this point, all our kids trusted our responses and reactions to their beliefs and would talk to us about anything. We wanted to protect that, even if it meant taking risks. We were scared LK might succumb to drug use and fall into a lifestyle that would lead her down a road without purpose and pursuit of God. Added to our fear was the pain we experienced seeing LK face some hurtful comments from others around her. All we could do was hurt for our daughter. It was as if she was in the rapids of a river, about to go over the falls, and we couldn't get to her.

Eventually the relationship with Rachel fell apart. Rachel gave up and slowly disappeared. But even after she was gone, the experiences with Rachel had deeply imprinted LK, and she was living an identity we hadn't expected. The whole ordeal radically impacted our family.

It's hard to put into words on a page how much I (we) love and respect LK. She's one of the strongest women I know, and she is deeply passionate and caring. Many times, her opinions help me see my own errors in thinking, and so LK is someone I listen to, even when I disagree with her. I am confident she will always make it in this world and will impact those around her because she fiercely loves those who are loyal to her. Her heart, combined with her opinions, means she will resolutely stand up for the less fortunate. Her feminist ideals, combined with her deep love for Jesus, fuel her equal treatment of people. She's the Samaritan—she stops for others. Having Little Kitty as my daughter, and her openness about her sexual identity, has shaped me as a pastor, a dad, and a human. She has helped me think outside the religion box and to see the world as a place to voice your heart and opinion in a loving way, all to make it a better place to live for everyone. Because of her, I see how important it is for our feelings and identity to be transparent, that we are on a journey and should live honestly with other people. I love her deeply, and God does too. I am better because of her!

Even though God gives good lessons out of hard seasons of life, our experiences with this family left some splinters in us. We still feel them at times. It's that feeling you have when you think you've got the splinter out, but it feels like there's something still there. You can't figure out if it's just a memory pain, or if a little piece is still lodged in there. Whatever it is, sometimes we talk about that period and the tears help lubricate the splinter and it quits hurting as much. Perhaps it will always be in there. I've come to think that our journey with this particular family, and with Rachel, continues to shape our own bravery to walk where God asks us to go, even when we don't feel up to it. I think the feeling of a constant splinter reminds us that we can walk through hard places if we stay close to Jesus. We've made other hard decisions to join God on mission, and somehow I think we felt prepared because of this specific experience. It trained us to take risks. It trained us to walk with a cross.

Many people view our engagement with Linda as a mistake: we should have left them on their side of the tracks and continued our lives, without pain and turbulence. Kitty and I prefer to see these moments as links in a chain, where with each link a person gets closer and closer to Jesus. Each experience teaches us a new and different thing about Jesus as well as about ourselves. For the Lindas we come in contact with, perhaps it's the link that brings them to actually following Jesus. Experiences like this certainly keep *us* closer to following him, because without him, we could never do it.

The journey of carrying a cross won't always work out perfectly, but it teaches us to depend on God, and to take hold of different disciplines, ones that involve practice, risk, and adventure.

Our son Will asked Kitty, "Momma, does it discourage you when you do all this stuff for people and don't see them change?" Kitty answered, "Yes, sometimes it does, but then I remember that I'm being obedient to Jesus and may be part of someone's 'pre-Jesus' journey." Kitty might have said, "We're just carrying our cross daily, and sometimes we get splinters."

The Forgotten Practices

The rhythms of cultural church life today were birthed out of a good place. In wanting to "practice" their faith, the early church continued disciplines and rhythms of faith from Jesus and the Scriptures, with the goal of developing habits that would help them to follow God. "Practice" is the engine of rhythm, especially in faith. Even other religions will engage with various disciplines or practices for deepening faith. "Practicing" your faith is also something that can delineate people who exhibit rhythms of faith from those who don't. Sometimes you'll hear Jews speak of being a "practicing" Jew, or Catholics being a "practicing" Catholic, to differentiate from those who don't follow the rhythms of their faith. A person may still believe intellectually in the tenets of a particular faith, but they fail to live the rhythms prescribed by it, and so they are not viewed as "practicing." You will meet people all the time who believe in Jesus and God as a Creator but don't live out the practices or rhythms of a Christian's faith. On the other end of that spectrum, you will meet many people within Christianity who are diligent about many spiritual disciplines and rhythms that keep them centered on Jesus: a focused prayer life, regular church attendance, worship with other believers, observing the sacraments, and the study of the Scriptures. These "inward" practices are fuel for our internal connection to God and our unity as the church. They give us the centering of mind and soul that helps us live in a chaotic culture together as believers, keeping our focus on the kingdom and growing our connection with Jesus.

However, I wonder if we have lost sight of some additional and equally important spiritual practices (disciplines). We often talk of spiritual disciplines as a way to grow in Christ, but rarely are they focused outwardly toward other people. They seem to drive us toward a healthy vertical relationship to help us grow to "love God" as Jesus instructed, but they are rarely focused on "loving our neighbor" with the same intentionality. Outward disciplines are often considered an "add-on" to a healthy faith life.

While the internal practices that bring us knowledge as well as a sense of closeness to God are vitally important, a holistic rhythm of practices that also includes hospitality, feeding the poor, and embracing the marginalized of society seems to be left unsaid or merely given a footnote. James, the brother of Jesus, even proclaimed that pure and undefiled religion looked like taking care of the widows and orphans,[47] so surely our spiritual disciplines should include these types of practices. James even went so far as to define the authenticity of our faith by whether or not it is accompanied by action. Our faith is expressed in both belief *and* action.[48]

If we take the words of Jesus seriously then we should give equal focus to the outward practices of who we are as Christ-followers. While inward disciplines will help our heart and soul connect to our God, outward disciplines will help us see others as our God sees them.

Diana Butler Bass insists that, "Christian spirituality is grounded in imitation" and that our ultimate practices should be an imitation of Jesus and his life.[49] She adds that imitation is the most powerful way to learn practices. As followers of Jesus then, our practices should flow from our Teacher, our

---

47 James 1:27.
48 James 2:14–18.
49 Diana Butler Bass, *Christianity After Religion: The End of Church and the Birth of a New Spiritual Awakening* (New York: HarperOne, 2013), 184–185.

Rabbi, our Lord. These types of practices should be the natural outpouring of our focus on prayer, worship and study of the Scriptures. The inward disciplines that form our thought life, prayer life, and knowledge of God, should find their completion in actions towards others. To only practice part of the list, the "inside" list, is ultimately an unsatisfying and incomplete Christianity at best. A purposeful faith, filled with good inward spiritual disciplines, will produce a love for God and a heart that looks like his. The natural outpouring of that connection to God should be directed into other people's lives. This is how Jesus lived, every part of his incarnational filling resulting in a pouring out to touch others, eventually leading to his ultimate pouring out on the cross.

At lunch with author and speaker Reggie McNeal, we were talking about the story of the Good Samaritan, which we discussed earlier in this book. Reggie made the obvious, but less-talked-about point, that Jesus ended that discussion by saying, "Go and do likewise"(Luke 10:37).[50] He didn't tell him to go and learn more, go and worship more, go to more meetings…he told him to go and *be* the Samaritan. So we practice our faith that proclaims love for one another, love for our enemy, and love for our neighbor. Yes, practice "just being" in the presence of God (as Jesus did with the Father through inward focused prayer) but also practice being in the presence of your neighbor.

While there are some streams of Christianity and monastic communities that do focus on ethical practices, my years in the

---

50 From a dialogue with Reggie McNeal, used with permission.

evangelical world have shown me that living missionally, being the Samaritan, is a forgotten discipline. The truth is, a person's Christian life risks stalling without missional and ethical practices that launch them into other people's lives and journeys. When we seek to balance both internal and external disciplines and habits, we find a faith that becomes exhilarating and exciting, as the deeper connections to God overflow into the ways we love each other and our neighbor. As Michael Frost says, "The trick is to develop habits that both unite us together as believers, while also propelling us into the lives of others."[51]

It can be more comfortable to focus on internal disciplines. Adding disciplines that make us stop on the side of the road like the Samaritan can become really messy, but then we get to live a life out loud, alerting people to the kingdom of God and his redemptive story, joining God in his mission to love the world. To say that we must really feed the poor, or love our enemies, or be involved in chaotic lives, means we might just get splinters. We probably will. But then shouldn't we expect that if we're carrying a cross?

People of a God of Grace

When we begin to think about engaging the margins of society, or a family like Linda's, our natural response is, "How in the world can I be brave enough to do this?" To go from a religious practice that only involves Sunday morning attendance to living a life that's a bit louder, engaging in the lives of

---

51 Frost, *Surprise the World*, 22.

complex people, can absolutely involve some risk. It can feel like you're jumping a minibike over a dirt mound, not knowing how you'll land. But we must remember that these movements into imperfect life-journeys need not be in our own strength. There's a subtle shift in perspective, which can help us all walk the roads of messy living and missional practice: it's in knowing that we are not so much a people *of* grace, as we are a people of a *God of grace.*

A pastor friend of mine, Jonathan, helped me realize that the grace I give to others is not *my* grace to give: it's Jesus' grace, which I simply steward and carry for him as his disciple.[52] He is the one, through the Holy Spirit, who gives me the patience, bravery and strength to live into situations that are scary and beyond my own capacity to give. Showing people grace in my own strength can be daunting when faced with very messy situations. I know I'm supposed to give grace to people and not judge them, but when I look at others through my eyes, I rarely can find enough grace to give. The position may appear too difficult, too complicated, and there's some amount of judgment I seem to always carry into a situation. However, being a people of a God of grace means we rely on him to give his grace through us. We don't need to muster up the grace in our own strength. If we see grace as something that is his, and we simply carry it and give it to others, then the struggle of giving grace is put squarely where he wants it, on his shoulders, through his hands, on the cross he surrendered to.

---

52 Used with permission from conversations and sermons by Jonathan Cleveland.

Yes, being a people of a *God of grace* rather than a people *of* grace is far more than just semantics. It's a freeing shift in perspective. When you learn to walk as a carrier of the grace of God, you find a certainty that he is walking with you, into situations you would never get involved with on your own. On the other side of these sometimes difficult engagements with others, you see how the Holy Spirit uses you to transform lives, as well as seeing God transform you in the process.

My encouragement is that we quit trying to give people grace in our own strength. Simply give them God's grace... the same grace he gives us. It's hard to give people something you wouldn't normally have for them. It's much easier to give them something we already have, because it's been given to us by God.

We can certainly walk into church, feed on the information given from the stage, and only connect with our small group or Bible study friends. But we will miss out on a bigger life—a life out loud! We will miss out on the splinters, the transforming adventure God invites us into. Sure, keeping to ourselves hurts less, but it's also a stagnant, quiet life. As we carry our cross and live into other people's lives, we will inevitably get splinters. But Jesus promises if we lose our life for his sake, we will find it.[53] The splinters you get will accompany stories that make your life meaningful, adventurous and will enliven your faith. You won't be alone, because you'll be following Jesus. The truth is, living a comfortable

---

53 Matthew 16:25.

life, where faith is only defined by church membership and activities, ironically means you've left the path that Jesus walked. He walked, ate, and hung out with sinners, prostitutes, and social misfits. So join him not only at church gatherings, but join him outside the walls of the church building, and you'll meet the same people he did. Expect splinters, but remember, Jesus received the worst splinters of all from a cross. Carrying a cross, hanging on a cross, gave Jesus splinters, and will give you splinters as well.

Splinters accompany loving people and living out loud.

ONE LOUDER STEP

Ask the Holy Spirit to identify a relationship, possibly a difficult one, where you should live more intentionally as a Christ-follower. Expect splinters, but live and walk the same road that Jesus did in carrying a cross. Seek relationship over the expectation that they will agree with your belief system.

8

Beyond the Holodeck

Walk into the local big-box electronics store these days and you can find technology we could only dream of a few years ago. Virtual reality glasses and goggles have become readily available. These mobile projection units visually create a whole new three-dimensional reality, allowing you to become some-*one* else, some*where* else. You can fly the Millennium Falcon as Han Solo, glide through the air as Wonder Woman, or whizz up a skyscraper as Spider-Man. I can only imagine where this technology will be in twenty years, or one hundred years!

One of my all-time favorite shows is *Star Trek*. I wouldn't say I'm an official Trekkie, but I do have opinions as to which captain was best and which Enterprise season was superior. One of the best things about *Star Trek* was that the show was filled with devices and instruments from the imagined future.

The writers were always doing their best to forecast where technology might go. Perhaps my favorite technological forecast was the "holodeck." This was part of the series *Star Trek: The Next Generation*.[54] The holodeck was a room on the space craft Enterprise in which crew members could craft and dream up an alternate, virtual reality. If a crew member needed a recreational break, with one request to the computer they could be in a western town, complete with dusty streets, six guns and a saloon...even horses. If they wanted to be in a beautiful mountainscape, the holodeck could deliver. Sometimes the holodeck was even used to work out theories that would save the ship's engines or help them out of a predicament they couldn't figure out in reality. Then, if the engines blew up, it was just virtual; it wasn't real.

Perhaps holodecks and full-on virtual reality are not so far off in the future. Maybe we already have rooms where we talk and teach a lot about the kingdom and following Jesus, trying to work out what it might look like in reality. We enter a room and live out our faith mentally and verbally, but maybe never really take it into our everyday life. We talk about Jesus walking dusty roads and performing miracles, but we simply imagine it as the stuff of stories, the past, a time we don't have to worry about. We can nod our heads in agreement, but does what we hear really make it out into the roads of our neighborhood, or the halls of our workplace or school? Do we walk

---

54 *Star Trek: The Next Generation*, produced by Gene Roddenberry and Rick Berman, Paramount Domestic Television, 1987–1994, television series.

out of the holodeck and back into reality, carrying what we've learned into real life? Do we ever really follow Jesus outside the church walls?

Bringing the Tangible

Living a life that speaks out loud does not happen by accident. Sharing the gospel in everyday life is something we have to make space for, as we intentionally join God in bringing awareness of his presence into the places where we are present. Remember, God is already at work in a place or a person's life—we just join him in that work.

One of the most helpful books on intentional and missional living within a specific place is Alan Briggs' book *Staying Is the New Going*. In chapter three, Briggs gets us thinking about the history behind the place we inhabit. If it's a neighborhood, who has lived there the longest? What is the history of that place over time? What are the visible needs as you meet and learn to live with your neighbors? Alan suggests we can find our ministry strategy by looking intentionally at a place, neighborhood, workplace, or community.[55] As we become part of the ecosystem of that community, we find the places we can bring the kingdom to bear and show the love of Jesus in tangible ways. We start to see changes in other people's lives as we care for the "cracks" in the community pavement, as Briggs calls them.

As we discover the needs of a community system, one of

---

55 Alan Briggs, *Staying Is the New Going: Choosing to Love Where God Places You* (Colorado Springs: NavPress, 2015), 41–57.

the easiest ways to then build relationship is to invite others to join in the rebuilding and redemption of that need. You may discover a park that needs to be cleaned up. You may have coffee with the school principal and find out how you could help their staff or students. Or you might talk to the city board member for your area and see what the needs are in the neighborhood. It could involve hosting a BBQ and asking your neighbors what they would like to see come to fruition in the community; perhaps asking your work colleagues how they can have more fun or team building times after work. Whatever the space or the environment, God wants to use you to bring the kingdom into the hearing and viewing of others. It may start as simply as Jesus started, with food around a table, walking the streets of your neighborhood, engaging others in their own community space.

Hugh Halter and Matt Smay say in their book, *The Tangible Kingdom*:

> We have to remember that the ancient faith communities that set a course to change the history of the world did so without church programs, without paid staff, without web sites, and without brochures, blogs, or buildings. They were lean! The point of going without all the stuff is simple but profound. When you don't have all the "stuff," you're left with a lot of time to spend with people.[56]

---

56 Hugh Halter and Matt Smay, *The Tangible Kingdom: Creating Incarnational Community* (San Francisco: Jossey-Bass, 2008), 25.

Often, the gospel and the kingdom of God are best shared life on life, through relationship. Tangibly showing what the gospel is can take time. Regular cookouts with neighbors might be the beginning of a conversation about the kingdom of God that doesn't lead to following Jesus for several months, or years. Your presence in the neighborhood as a representative of God's kingdom might take a long, consistent involvement before you're ever asked about Jesus. The point is that evangelism and announcing the kingdom can take on many forms and shapes, not just verbal preaching or teaching. And, while the kingdom can be talked about in the holodeck sanctuary, it shows up in reality by the way you live and walk among others.

Pancakes on the Porch

One couple I know moved into their neighborhood and decided to be the gathering point for their neighbors. They left the holodeck and took their knowledge about Jesus and joined him outside the church walls. They wanted to build relational community in their neighborhood and visibly live out the gospel. Kevin and Lydia started by inviting people to a monthly event called Pancakes on the Porch. Now, one Saturday morning per month over the summer, some twenty to forty people will walk down the street and gather in their front yard, as pancakes, bacon, and other goodies are prepared.[57] Everyone chips in, and they all gather to connect and be part of each

---

57 To see this in action, see "Pancakes on the Porch Pulpit Rock," https://vimeo.com/291828925 (last accessed November 19, 2018).

other's lives. It's a simple and fun way for Kevin and Lydia to communicate to their neighbors, "You matter to us." One of their neighbors told me when I visited, "When Kevin and Lydia moved into the neighborhood, they just started drawing everyone toward their house and front porch." This is intentional and missional living, where your place matters, and the people who share your place also matter. Will it lead to people following Jesus? I hope so, and know they do too, but they live this way because Jesus lived this way, no matter the end result. To be a disciple is to imitate him, and that's enough of a reason.

Brad Brisco and Lance Ford remind us that one of the first miracles children often learn about is the feeding of the five thousand, and that after that, we see numerous pictures of Jesus around the table with food, talking about what the kingdom really looks like. Brisco and Ford suggest that if you bumped into Jesus on the streets you'd probably need to invite him to a BBQ instead of a Bible study, that while churches are often found meeting, Jesus was found eating.[58] It might be a BBQ, it might be pancakes, or it might be sushi. Sometimes it might not involve food. But it will always involve sharing our life in some way, rather than just inviting people to a church event. This can be as easy as meeting together at a park, or engaging other parents at the kids' soccer game, or maybe just gathering at your house. As the relationships grow and the community builds, then you will find places to live your

---

58 Brad Brisco and Lance Ford, *Next Door as It Is in Heaven: Living out God's Kingdom in Your Neighborhood* (Colorado Springs: NavPress, 2016),110.

life as an example of the kingdom of God. You may even get the chance to share about it verbally. By demonstrating the gospel in tangible ways, you'll find your life is all of a sudden a little louder.

Tiny Houses and Loud Living

I had the privilege of staying at Community First Village in Austin, TX. When you drive into Community First you wonder if you're driving into a mobile home park on steroids. There are permanently installed RV trailers everywhere, along with tiny houses of all kinds. There's an outdoor movie amphitheater, a barber shop, a store, a community garden, and my favorite part—goats and chickens. Community First Village is the ambition of a man named Alan Graham who dreamed of providing housing and, more importantly, community to every homeless person in Austin.[59] What has been created at Community First is nothing short of remarkable. When you walk down the main street, "Goodness Way," into the Village, you see and meet people who love each other, who have found a place to belong, and have purpose in life. We were told the story of one man who held up the key to his tiny house and remarked, "I've never owned keys before." People find self-worth at Community First Village and they find each other.

Those who are homeless can apply for housing in the community through various avenues. If accepted, they get their own tiny house, or a couple gets a camper. They automatical-

---

59 Community First Village, https://mlf.org/community-first/ .

ly become part of a community that has numerous resources, events, a garden where residents can grow some of their own food, an art program, a mechanic shop, and other community-giving projects. The Village also offers help in life-skill areas, such as addiction recovery and literacy. I immediately noticed they live in close proximity, sharing kitchens, picnic areas, and beautifully maintained common areas. The homeless find a home, but as one staff member told us, "The real thing they find is community." For Alan Graham, Community First Village was his way of living out loud, moving an idea from the holodeck of his sanctuary to real life. And now it's become a place where others can live out loud and move into reality with each other.

However, with community comes messiness. On our tour of the twenty-seven-acre facility, we were told numerous stories of the issues surrounding complex and chaotic lives. People on the street have usually faced multiple physical and emotional hardships and as a result might carry some baggage, addictions, and relational brokenness (not that we all don't carry issues). And so, when these people live in community, it can bring additional challenges, additional splinters. In a beautiful example of kingdom living, staff have chosen to work at the Village, and couples and families have opted to live in a tiny house, alongside their hurting Austin residents from the streets. It's costly, but they also reap the rewards of joining God in redeeming lives and being part of stories that are examples of rescue and transformation.

People learn to live intentionally at Community First Village. This is a skill and discipline we often lack in our everyday lives. We are so accustomed to pulling into our driveways, raising the garage door, driving our car in, then dropping the door behind us, that we forget to be intentional with our neighbors and those we live with. In the Village there are no garages. Front porches of tiny houses often face other front porches. Life is shared as residents garden together, bump into each other on the roads of the Village, join in activities, or just experience the new joy of community together.

During my time at Community First Village it struck me that many people on the outside of the Village, with their lives "put together", suffer the same major symptom the homeless did before they arrived: *a lack of intentional community*. Sometimes we can assume we live in a community because we own a house smack dab in the middle of other houses. However, proximity doesn't guarantee community. Many of us can't even name the neighbors on either side of us or across the street.

What if we were the catalysts on our street to begin a Community First Village mentality? Might we find what the homeless have found at the Village? They found more than a roof over their head: they found other people on the journey with them. They found more than a cure for physical homelessness: they found community. It's human nature to pick and choose our friends. We find people who make us comfortable and lean into relationships that seem fulfilling, but what if we lived counterculturally and dug deeply into other people's lives, people we might not naturally choose as friends? It's easy to give grace to those we like and agree with. It's much harder to love people we don't agree with, or are uncomfortable with. This becomes a reality at the Village.

In Luke's Gospel, Jesus says:

> "If you love those who love you, what credit is that to you? Even sinners love those who love them. And if you do good to those who are good to you, what credit is that to you? Even sinners do that. And if you lend to those from whom you expect repayment, what credit is that to you? Even sinners lend to sinners, expecting to be repaid in full. But love your enemies, do good to them, and lend to them without expecting to get anything back. Then your reward will be great, and you will be children of the Most High, because he is kind to the ungrateful and wicked. Be merciful, just as your Father is merciful."
>
> LUKE 6:32–36

When we intentionally love people we don't get along with, don't agree with, or don't have commonality with, Jesus says we're being merciful just as God is merciful to us. We may not get paid back, but this is our calling as missional people, carrying glimpses of the kingdom into other people's lives.

We deliberately look for places we can live out of our own comfort zone and into the place where we need God to walk with us.

You have complete freedom to stay behind closed doors and limit your tribe to the people you are most comfortable with. But the risk is that you'll miss out on joining God in the adventure outside the holodeck sanctuary. A loud life will live into all the spaces you work and live and will not just impact your friends, but will be heard in all aspects of your life.

Social Justice: Running into the Plague

I think it's important in our discussions of missional living and demonstrating the kingdom that we, at least briefly, discuss social justice in the context of following Jesus.

I find it sad that the church often debates the need for focusing on social justice issues. Somehow we have dismissed clean water, equal rights, and social concerns as unnecessary, unless accompanied with verbal presentations. As with the early church, history can be written with a defining pen of grace if we will just take up the challenge to lean into hard social discourse and involvement with no agenda other than simply being the heart of God for people. Social justice is a prime place to join arms with others and find a common mission of redeeming people's lives. We can invite non-followers into kingdom work, or just join them in their work, and find common goals to redeem people and creation. Frost puts this into perspective for us:

There is no longer any need to debate whether
we prefer evangelism or social justice. There is
no need to argue which is primary and which
creates a platform for the other. This debate
about hierarchy is redundant. We should not
be committed to social action purely as a means
to create opportunities to do the "real mission"
of evangelism[...]We are called to alert people
to the reign and rule of God through Christ,
and this will involve being [people] that both
demonstrate (justice, love, reconciliation) and
announce (heralding, worship, evangelism)
that reign.[60]

The point is that we can both *proclaim* the reign of God, his
kingdom, and also *show* it in tangible ways through social
justice, eating together, simple acts of kindness and redemption. We need not use one as a ploy for the other, and we need
not lead with a sermon on how salvation is found. The invitation is not just for salvation—it's to join God's kingdom, which
is much more beautiful and grand.

As we look for ways to live into broken places and show
the kingdom of God, we will begin to see natural opportunities
to help bring restoration. Faith-based organizations commonly
take action to feed the poor in a city. We often see initiatives
to fight sex trafficking, or to provide solutions to foster care
and adoption. All around the world, both faith-based and

---

60 Michael Frost, *The Road to Missional* (Grand Rapids: Baker Books, 2011), 29–30.

non-faith-based organizations and individuals are working to bring clean water and healthcare to those in need. These types of social concerns intersect our so-called sacred and secular belief systems. We can partner with those who don't claim allegiance to Jesus but are actually feeling the draw as *imago Dei* to bring restoration and healing to others in need. Though they might not see themselves as an agent of God, we all have the same call to "good deeds." In these partnerships for good, both groups want to see the hungry fed, the sick healed, the broken restored. These are not just human good deeds, they look very much like Jesus' ministry on earth. When the church proactively gets involved with issues of social justice, it shows that the kingdom doesn't just exist in a book, in a holodeck. It shows that there are Jesus people who believe the kingdom exists in reality. Often in these intersections of common good, we have opportunity for winsome conversations about God and how our partnered mission is an example of his kingdom.

In fact, the church had some of its growth booms from living into social justice during the plagues of early civilization. The Plague of Cyprian, in the years from AD 250–270, devastated the Roman Empire by taking up to 5000 lives per day at times. The event was chronicled by St. Cyprian, whom it was named after. It was during this time that Christians were also persecuted empire-wide by Emperor Decius. Despite this persecution, the Christians were known for caring for those who were dying around them, running into the plague rather than away from it. Their "questionable lives" ended up catching the curiosity of their pagan neighbors. A century earlier, Christians had responded in a similar fashion during the Antonine Plague.[61]

The church's legacy is of being a people who run into the places where society is hurting, screaming, and sometimes dying. How is it that social justice has become something only the political left does, instead of it being a kingdom way of living out loud? For the church to be heard, we must live a louder presence, and run into the plague of life to heal and love people the way the early church did…the way Jesus did.

Escapism

There is no doubt we have a future that points to more and more virtual reality options. According to tech leaders, the possibilities are endless: "One could have breakfast at the Louvre beside the Winged Victory of Samothrace, followed by a lunchtime spelunk through Thailand's water caves."[62] Mark Zuckerberg, the founder of Facebook, says "One day, we believe this kind of immersive, augmented reality will become a part of daily life for billions of people."[63] Most researchers, even if they disagree with the speed and depth of virtual reality social addictions, agree that there are negative side-effects of escapism. The faux reality offered through such technology

61 https://www.biblicalarchaeology.org/daily/ancient-cultures/daily-life-and-practice/the-antonine-plague-and-the-spread-of-christianity/ .

62 Monica Kim, "The Good and The Bad of Escaping to Virtual Reality," *The Atlantic*, February 18, 2015. https://www.theatlantic.com/health/archive/2015/02/the-good-and-the-bad-of-escaping-to-virtual-reality/385134/ .

63 Ibid.

artificially feeds our needs for identity, significance, and connectivity, while remedying the risks and vulnerability associated with real relationships and social interaction.

Ernest Cline's popular book turned movie, *Ready Player One,* offers an interesting social commentary on this very issue.[64] In the story, we enter a world built on people living pseudo realities and identities within the diasporic culture in which they live. The key characters have little validation in the real world, and so they seek purpose and adventure by entering an alter-world where they live an identity that brings value, community, and meaning.

I wonder if in the church we haven't built, even unintentionally, a type of escapism, where the words of Jesus, "Go and do likewise," have been replaced with, "Come and hear, come and sing." Are we possibly caught in a whirlpool that keeps us circling the words of Jesus to love our neighbor, without actually ever reaching the center of the message? We imagine what that looks like as we sit in neatly lined rows and respond affirmatively to, "Can I get an amen?" The canon of Scripture was never meant to create a virtual reality for us to simply study. It was never meant to help us escape the realities of the culture and the world. The Bible is a pathway to live into reality, to live a life out loud, much like the God-following communities written about in the pages themselves. Please, let the Bible come alive! We are meant to live free of virtual

---

64 Ernest Cline, *Ready Player One* (Arrow, 2012), directed by Steven Spielberg, Warner Bros. Pictures, 2018, film.

reality goggles that mask our sight from culture around us. We are not to seek an escape, but to lean into reality. *Incarnation is to have flesh on, not goggles.*

I want to encourage you to take the VR goggles off your faith, the things we nod our head to and murmur "Amen." Take a walk across the street, to the cubicle down the row, sit in the other bleachers at soccer practice, seek out an encounter with others. Live into incarnation, not fantasy. When you play "for real," you'll find your Sunday morning experiences are much more meaningful. You'll suddenly realize you've left the holodeck, and entered a whole new world. The *real* world.

The Future Starts Now

One of the tenets of our Christian faith is the hope of eternal life. However, when we get caught up in primarily living toward the future reality of heaven and eternity, we can lose sight of the kingdom now. Our preaching, our studies, and our gatherings can so often be forward-focused, to the life-after, that we forget our identity now as Christ-followers. We can find ourselves prioritizing getting people across a salvation line and into the heaven of the future, but then fall short of inviting them into the kingdom now, which includes redemption, grace, beauty, and mercy for *today*. We sing about where we're going with no sense that we are alive in the present! The future is now, according to the Apostle Peter:

> What a God we have! And how fortunate we
> are to have him, this Father of our Master Jesus!

Because Jesus was raised from the dead, we've been given a brand-new life and have everything to live for, including a future in heaven—and the future starts now!

1 PETER 1:3–4 (MSG)

The invitation for God's kingdom starts now! We are invited to join Jesus in his kingdom work now, working alongside him in redeeming his creations and creation. It's the invitation to live into reality rather than being stuck in a virtual existence. Even though the world we live in is broken and incomplete, we give glimpses of the age to come by the way we live within our culture and society, by the ways we love our neighbor.

In addition to the glorious gift of salvation, we can live out and announce the pivotal and foundational constructs of the kingdom that Jesus proclaimed himself:

"Blessed are the poor in spirit,
    for theirs is the kingdom of heaven.
Blessed are those who mourn,
    for they will be comforted.
Blessed are the meek,
    for they will inherit the earth.
Blessed are those who hunger and thirst
    for righteousness, for they will be filled.
Blessed are the merciful,
    for they will be shown mercy.

Blessed are the pure in heart,
for they will see God.
Blessed are the peacemakers,
for they will be called children of God.
Blessed are those who are persecuted because
of righteousness,
for theirs is the kingdom of heaven.
"Blessed are you when people insult you,
persecute you and falsely say all kinds of evil
against you because of me. Rejoice and be glad,
because great is your reward in heaven, for in
the same way they persecuted the prophets
who were before you."

MATTHEW 5:3–12

When Jesus came on the scene, this was the kingdom he was ushering in. These "Beatitudes" are the manifesto for a life out loud. The kingdom shows up now in the blessings we carry when we show mercy to those who need it, give voice to those who experience meekness, teach those who thirst for righteousness, or lift up those who are poor in spirit.

So let's join Jesus outside the walls of the church, in the places we live, work, and play. Go for the real-life adventure beyond the holodeck. Be the kingdom, tell of the kingdom, and demonstrate the kingdom.

ONE LOUDER STEP

Practice Jesus' command to "Love your neighbor as yourself." Begin doing small acts of love towards those in your neighborhood and workplace, the employee at the grocery checkout, the teachers at your child's school, and others you come in contact with. Live the gospel, outside of Sunday church.

Conclusion: 165 Hours

So we've come to the end of the book, and in my experience, there are a few ways this can now go. I've been at this very point hundreds of times throughout my years of reading! Books with stories like this one might pull on your heartstrings; they might bring really good intentions to the surface of your life; they may have even led you to highlight some points in the chapters. But often they are given a firm closing of the last page, a smile, a nod of the head and a, "Wow, that was good." If that is your verdict, then thank you. Some would say I have done my job well if this book stays out on your coffee table or bed stand where it's accessible, or the corners of the pages are dog-eared and the outer cover is worn from being folded back. For an author, worn corners are a great compliment indeed! However, I have a different measurement of success. I want to ask you to think hard about something and not just rush through this conclusion.

From my perspective, I will have succeeded if you feel led to get up from your pew, your normal chair in church and add to that experience, *a louder life*. I don't want you to *leave* your church community. I'm really hoping you feel the need to gather with your community each Sunday or Saturday, or whatever day you meet. But, let's not fall into the trap of defining our Christian faith by that one hour a week we gather inside a building for teaching, singing and sacraments. Some of us may also serve in other ministry activities during that gathering and so might spend three hours that define our "ministry" each week. This is good! Keep doing it! However, our church gathering should equip us and propel us *out* into the world in which Jesus *sent* us, helping us focus on how we live the other 165 hours a week, the places we inhabit with our life. It's in these places Jesus walked when he was on earth, and it's to these places you and I have been sent today to announce and demonstrate the kingdom of God. You'll find Jesus at work in these places just as much, if not more, than in the walls of the church.

What I hope you see now is that Jesus *has* invited you to participate in his mission, a life out loud! Jesus has already called you to step out of the room and be "sent" as he told those early disciples behind locked doors. If you decide to live this way, go purchase a new journal or notebook right now, for the stories you collect will start filling the pages, and you'll want to reread them over and over again. You'll need a place on your wall for a picture of Larry. You'll need more chairs around your table as stories invade your dining space. You'll need a BBQ grill for your porch as neighbors find their way to your house.

If you feel a desire to stop running on a hamster wheel of religion, or if you need to find something more to energize your normal church rhythms, put your ear to the wind, and you might just hear that the kingdom is calling you now. The voice you will hear is God's call for you to join him in his work of announcing Jesus to the rest of the world. It sounds much like, "Come, follow me..."

Jesus invites you to so much more than church attendance.

> He invites you to put on Will's eyes.
> He invites you to smell like the gospel.
> He invites you to season the world around you with good taste.
> He invites you to be involved in other people's messy lives.
> Yes, you might get hit on the field of play.
> Yes, you might get splinters carrying a cross.
> Seeing people first as images of God may feel uncomfortable.
> Putting away judgment will be hard yet rewarding.
> Stepping out of the holodeck and into reality might take bravery.

But when you start changing your perspective, and begin asking more daring questions that lead you into the streets where Jesus lives, you will find an incredibly meaningful faith, where you work side by side with God in bringing people hope, healing, and justice. Doesn't that sound like a better way? Doesn't that sound like *life*?

If Jesus appeared to you right now, in the room where you

are reading this, and said, "Get up, open the door and go out. As the Father has sent me so I am sending you," what would your next steps be? How would you determine a path to being "sent?" To whom are you sent?

Here are some obvious places to start:

1. Begin praying that the Holy Spirit would lead you into a life as a sent person.
2. Become intentional in looking for places to see people, notice people, and love them (make little notes or reminders if it helps).
3. Invite your neighbors for a meal and see where it goes.
4. Look for ways you can help redeem people's struggles or be a support in their life.
5. Become *active* the other 165 hours of the week!

There are additional resources listed in the next section to help you on this journey. Take advantage of them, read them, join a tribe of people like Forge. Contact me if you need help in finding a Forge tribe near you.

If we are to be complete in our faith, then we must follow Jesus and his example. We cannot imitate Jesus and separate the announcement of God's reign from its demonstration. And so, I invite you to join me on the field and *demonstrate* the things we learn from great sermons, or from our own study and examination of Jesus' life. If you're sitting in the pew, bored, waiting to play, God has already invited you to get up and claim your own thrilling life following Jesus. It's yours, so live it.

A life out loud!

Further Resources

The resources that follow are designed to help you find a path and engagement in the concepts presented in this book. This is by no means an exhaustive list, but one I suggest as a starting point. I encourage you to seek a tribe like Forge America to continue your journey. In fact, I officially invite you to join us at Forge as we learn and walk as missional Jesus people together. Please feel free to contact me if you need assistance, have questions, or would value more conversation around these topics and your own life out loud.

May God bless you, challenge you, and bring you more life on your journey!

Get in Touch

- www.RowlandSmith.net
- https://redskies.blog
- rowland@forgeCOS.com
- 303-883-9002
- @Rowland_L_Smith
- Rowland.smith.549
- rowland_smith_62

For bulk/discount purchases of this book, please contact me directly.

Websites

The Forge tribe (Training in missional practices in the places you live, work, and play)
Colorado: www.forgeCOS.com
United States: www.forgeamerica.com
Outside USA: www.forgeinternational.com

100 Movements: (Catalyzing organizations and providing resources for missional movement)
www.100movements.com

Further Reading to Continue this Conversation

Staying Is the New Going by Alan Briggs (NavPress, 2015)
Christianity after Religion by Diana Butler Bass (HarperOne, 2013)
Next Door as It Is in Heaven by Lance Ford and Brad Brisco (NavPress, 2016)
Keep Christianity Weird by Michael Frost (NavPress, 2018)
Surprise the World by Michael Frost (NavPress, 2016)
The Road to Missional by Michael Frost (Baker Books, 2011)
The Shaping of Things to Come by Michael Frost and Alan Hirsch (Baker Books, 2013)
Love Does by Bob Goff (Thomas Nelson, 2012)
Untamed by Alan and Debra Hirsch (Baker Books, 2010)
Redeeming Sex by Debra Hirsch (IVP, 2015)
Love Is an Orientation by Andrew Marin (IVP, 2009)

About the Author

Rowland Smith is a missional practitioner and trainer, and is director of the Forge Colorado Springs hub, as well as serving on the Forge America National Team. He is the pastor of missional culture at Pulpit Rock Church, Colorado Springs and also helps lead Ecclesia Colorado Springs, a missional faith community. Rowland has a degree from Fuller Seminary in missiology and theology. He and his wife, Kitty, own Third Space Coffee, a missional café business model. They have one teenager, three adult children, and four dogs.

MOVEMENTS
PUBLISHING

100 Movements Publishing is a hybrid publisher, offering the benefits of both traditional and self-publishing.

OUR AUTHORS ARE **RISK-TAKERS**, **PARADIGM-SHIFTERS**, **INCARNATIONAL MISSIONARIES**, AND **INFLUENTIAL LEADERS** WHO LOVE THE BODY OF CHRIST AND WANT TO SPUR HER ON FOR MORE.

Our books aim to inspire and equip disciples to take hold of their God-given call to make disciples and to see kingdom impact in every sphere of society.

Changing the Conversation

OUR BOOKS SHIFT PARADIGMS, EQUIP LEADERS, AND INSPIRE MISSIONAL DISCIPLES TO PLAY THEIR PART IN CATALYZING MISSIONAL MOVEMENTS.

For more information please visit us at 100Mpublishing.com

CPSIA information can be obtained
at www.ICGtesting.com
Printed in the USA
FSHW012054020319

9 780998 639345